ParaPro Assessment Preparation (2019-2020)

A Complete Study Guide with 100+ Practice Test Questions For the ETS Praxis Paraprofessional Test

Copyright 2018 by ParaPro Test Prep Team - All rights reserved.

This publication is sold with the idea that the publisher is not required to render any accounting, officially or otherwise, or any other qualified services. If further advice is necessary, contacting a legal and/or financial professional is recommended.

-From a Declaration of Principles that was accepted and approved equally by a Committee of the American Bar Association and a Committee of Publishers' Associations.

In no way is it legal to reproduce, duplicate, or transmit any part of this document, either by electronic means, or in printed format. Recording this publication is strictly prohibited, and any storage of this document is not allowed unless with written permission from the publisher. All rights reserved.

The information provided herein is stated to be truthful and consistent, in that any liability, in terms of inattention or otherwise, by any usage or abuse of any policies, processes, or directions contained within, is the solitary and utter responsibility of the recipient reader. Under no circumstances will any legal responsibility or blame be held against the publisher for any reparation, damages, or monetary loss due to the information herein, either directly or indirectly.

Respective authors own all copyrights not held by the publisher.

The information herein is offered for informational purposes solely, and is universally presented as such. The information herein is also presented without contract or any type of guarantee assurance.

The trademarks presented are done so without any consent, and this publication of the trademarks is without permission or backing by the trademark owners. All trademarks and brands within this book are thus for clarifying purposes only and are the owned by the owners themselves, and not affiliated otherwise with this document.

Table of Contents

Notice **15**

Introduction **16**

    Understanding the Paraprofessional's Role 17

    About the Test 18

Section 1: Reading **20**

    Identifying the Three Parts of a Passage 20

        Main Idea 20

        Organization of Supporting Details 21

        Problem and Solution 23

        Keywords 24

    Meanings of Words and Phrases in Context 25

    Inferences or Implications 25

    Fact or Opinion 26

    Interpreting Information from Visual Data 27

    Phonics 28

    Breaking Words into Parts 29

    Compound Words 29

    Syllables 30

    Synonyms, Antonyms and Homonyms 30

Alphabetizing Words 31
Three Stages to Teach the Alphabet 31
Helping Students Use Reading Strategies 31
Flyover 32
Skimming 32
Scanning..33
Tentative Summary 34
Opening and Closing Sentences In a Paragraph 34
Signal Words 34
Understanding the Author's Intention 35
Emotional Words..35
Building Anticipation for the Content 36
Asking Questions to Gauge Understanding 36
Reading an Index 37
Assessing a Student's Ability to Understand the Text 38
Using a Dictionary..39
Interpreting Written Directions.....................................39
Statements that Agree or Disagree 40
Notes on the Testing Process 40
Reading Questions 42

Section 2: Writing 54

What You Will Be Tested On 54

Parts of Speech 54

    Noun 54

    Verb 55

    Adjective 55

    Adverb 56

    Preposition 58

    Conjunctions 58

    Interjections 58

The Use of Clauses 59

    Independent and Dependent Clauses 59

    Adverb Clauses 59

    Adjective Clause 59

    Simple and Complex Sentences 59

Subject and Predicate 60

Grammar 61

    Subject-Verb Agreement 61

    Verb Tense 61

    Noun-Pronoun Agreement 62

Parallelism 62

Agreement 62

Referring to an Institution 63

Gerunds 63

Word Usage 64

Point of View 65

First Person 65

Second Person 65

Third Person... 65

Use of Commas 66

Clauses and Conjunctions 66

Introductory Phrases 66

Adverbs.. 66

Separating Items 67

Adding Non-Essential Data 67

Comma Splice Error 67

Use of a Semicolon 68

Use of the Apostrophe... 68

Possession 68

Plural Possessives 68

Possessive Personal Pronouns 69

The Rules of Spelling 69
- Plural Forms 69
- Homonyms 70
- Suffixes 70
- Verbs Ending in Y 70
- Double Consonants 70
- Spelling Rules for Vowels 71
- Silent E 71
- Additional Spelling Rules 71

Quotations 72

Using References 72

Applying Writing Skills in the Classroom 73
- Planning the Project 73
- Defining the Topic 74
- Defining the Purpose 74
- Writing Modes 75
- Determining the Audience 76
- Prewriting 77
- Using Reference Materials 78
- Writing a Thesis Statement 79
- Proper Paragraphs 80

When to Divide Paragraphs 81

Planning Transitions 81

Using a Scholarly Approach to Writing 83

Active and Passive Voice 83

Using the Word 'It' 84

Creating a Conclusion 85

Drafting, Editing and Revising 86

Considerations for Revision 86

Revising for Focus 86

Revising to Strengthen a Statement 87

Revising Grammatical Errors 87

Making an Argument 87

Common Types of Arguments 88

Three Elements of an Argument 88

Fallacies 88

Completing the Writing Portion of the Test 90

Spelling Questions 90

Parts of Speech Questions 90

Sentence Analysis Questions 91

Reviewing Parts of a Sentence 91

Writing Questions 92

Section 3: Mathematics 102

Types of Numbers 102

Integers 102

Critical Numbers 104

Decimal Point 104

Positioning of Numbers (Place Value) 104

Basic Mathematics Functions 106

Addition 106

Subtraction 107

Multiplication and Multiplication Tables 107

Division 109

Odd and Even Numbers in Addition and Multiplication 109

Signed Numbers in Multiplication and Division 110

Advanced Math Functions 110

Decimals 110

Exponents 111

Radicands and Square Roots 112

Cubes 112

Fractions 112

Equivalent Fractions 113

    Multiplying Fractions 113

    Adding and Subtracting Fractions 113

Percentages 114

Estimation 115

Mean, Median and Mode.. 116

Order of Operations.. 117

Advanced Sequences... 119

Identifying Mathematical Symbols 120

Basic Math Terms 120

Solving Word Problems 121

Algebra 122

    Linear Equations 122

Inequalities.. 123

Representing Time.. 124

Representing Money 126

Converting Measures 127

    Metric System 128

    Metric System Prefixes 129

Geometry 130

    Shapes... 130

    Polygons.. 130

Angles 131

Triangle 132

Quadrilateral 132

Circles and Circular Measurements 133

Three-Dimensional Shapes 134

Concave 135

Regular Polygons 135

Polygon Measurements 136

Area 136

Surface Area 136

Volume 138

Coordinates 139

Parallel and Perpendicular Lines 140

The Value of π and its Use in Circular Measurements
.... 140

Intepreting Charts and Graphs 141

Bar Graph 141

Line Graph 142

Pie Chart 143

Identifying Trends on Charts and Graphs 144

Tables 145

Teaching Math Skills in the Classroom **145**

    Identify the Need 145

    Step by Step 146

    Recognize the Context 147

    Help Students Learn What Numbers to Focus on in Calculations 147

Completing the Math Test **147**

Math Questions **149**

Section 4: ParaPro Sample Test 160

Section 5: Additional Details 208

  Completing the Test **208**

    Managing Choices 208

    Review the Question Wording 209

    Questions on Visual Data or Readings 210

  Applying to Take a **211**

  Sending Test Results **211**

  Test Day **212**

  Scoring **213**

  Retaking the Test **214**

Conclusion 215

Notice

This book is a review of the ParaPro Assessment Test (ID #1755) as provided by ETS and Praxis. The questions included in this guide are illustrations and samples of what participants may encounter when completing the ParaPro test. Additional information on the test may be found at www.ets.org/praxis.

Introduction

Working as a paraprofessional can be one of the most rewarding tasks that you ever undertake. To enter the field, you have to prove your ability to help students grasp the many concepts they will encounter. The paraprofessional concepts focus both on knowing how to manage certain skills and educating students to follow them. This guide will provide you with information about the content of the official ParaPro test. This includes information on the reading, writing and mathematics segments of the test.

Completing and passing the test will allow you to be certified to work as a teaching assistant. This will help you when you're looking for employment at a school, particularly a primary school. Your work will focus on helping students learn while also assisting the primary teacher. Completing the ParaPro test will assess your understanding of children's learning processes and also provide you with the tools to assist children in learning. The test is divided into three segments with an emphasis on basic skills and application.

This guide focuses on three vital subjects: First, reading, reading comprehension and strategies for identifying content and details. Second, there is a section for writing that includes grammar, vocabulary, spelling, phonics, word usage, synonyms, antonyms, syllables, the parts of a sentence, vocabulary, phonics and strategies for outlining a document. Third, there is a segment on mathematics that concentrates on general mathematics including addition, subtraction and division of whole numbers; mixed numbers, fractions and decimal numbers; algebra, geometry and various other mathematical concepts.

This guide will help you properly prepare to take the ParaPro test. Among other topics, we will discuss timing so you can complete the test in the time allotted. What you learn here may also be carried over into the classroom as you educate students in any setting.

Understanding the Paraprofessional's Role

The ParaPro test is designed to help you enter the education sector. The test concentrates on the skills needed to be a paraprofessional, which is an educational assistant who offers specialized support to elementary and secondary students. The content assessed on the ParaPro test is focused on what you'll need to know in order to help students at these grade levels.

The role of a paraprofessional is to supplement the support that a teacher provides in the classroom. The paraprofessional will assist individual students with their work and offer assistance to the teacher as needed. In some cases, the paraprofessional may be available after school as a tutor for students who are struggling with certain concepts.

More importantly, a paraprofessional may help students who have special needs. It's often difficult for children with learning difficulties to keep up with the rest of the class. A paraprofessional will help such children by providing the extra support they need. Your work as a paraprofessional will make a true difference in the lives of those who most need help with their studies. This makes it all the more important for you to understand how to succeed on the ParaPro test.

About the Test

The ParaPro test is administered by the Educational Testing Service. It has been used since 2002 as a part of the United States' No Child Left Behind Act. The ParaPro test is one of three options that a person may choose to become certified as a paraprofessional. The other options are two years of college experience or earning an associate's degree. A person who has completed two or all three of these options may be more likely to find paraprofessional jobs, although the test itself is often seen as a necessity.

The ParaPro test has 90 questions divided into six segments divided evenly over the three concepts. The test includes the following segments:

1. Reading skills – 18 questions

2. Application of reading skills – 12 questions

3. Writing skills – 18 questions

4. Application of writing skills – 12 questions

5. Mathematics skills – 18 questions

6. Application of mathematics – 12 questions

The test assesses two main things. First, you must show that you understand the basic concepts that children need to learn in the classroom. The test content is detailed and specific, emphasizing a variety of topics which we will discuss in this book.

Second, you will have to show that you understand how to teach and assess students. Part of the task includes helping students to identify certain concepts.

This guide includes a series of sample questions that you may encounter in taking the actual ParaPro test. This includes a simulated version of the test. The questions in this book will not necessarily appear on the test. However, the content involved is presented in a way similar to what you might expect on the official test. You must review the content in each section of this guide to improve your chances of successfully passing the test.

In addition to the standard 90 questions on the ParaPro test, you may also be asked a few more which will not be graded. These questions are used to research possible questions that may be asked in future editions of the test.

You will be given 2.5 hours to complete the simulated test. A calculator may not be used during the math segment of the test. The actual ParaPro test may be computerized, although some groups may use paper tests depending on who is administering the test. The questions are generated at random through a computer program.

Section 1: Reading

The reading segment of this guide highlights principles of reading and how to help others who are learning to read or who want to improve upon their reading skills. Part of this includes reviewing how to identify the key parts of a passage, how to organize content, and comprehension, vocabulary and definitions. Types of words are also covered in this section.

Identifying the Three Parts of a Passage

When reading a passage, you will be tasked with identifying three important parts: the main idea, how the passage is organized and how certain ideas are related to each other, particularly the supporting details.

<u>Main Idea</u>

The main idea of a passage is the most important part of anything you are reading. It's the main message or key information the author is trying to convey. You can use the main idea to discover what a character is thinking. In other cases, you may be able to use the main idea to identify the writer's opinion.

In many cases, the main idea is at the very beginning in the first sentence. In other cases, you may find the main idea in the middle or end of the passage. The idea may not always be directly expressed.

To identify the main idea:

- Look for phrases such as "The most important thing to note is" or "The key purpose is."

- Look for specific examples tying into those phrases.
- Look for keywords such as "probably" or "in the future."
- Persuasive words like "ought" or "should" may also point you toward the main idea.

The main idea may be referenced many times within the passage. The writer may be trying to persuade the reader toward his or her viewpoint. The wording will be carefully chosen to support the main idea. The writer will reference that main idea repeatedly in order to reinforce a viewpoint and/or help people understand the main concept.

Another way to identify the main idea is to determine an author's purpose. This includes understanding what values that person has and whether an author is expressing facts or an opinion. Students should understand what the main idea is in order to have a better grasp of a passage's meaning.

Organization of Supporting Details

The supporting details in a passage link to the main idea that the writer is introducing. These details might provide the reader with factual information and definitions. The supporting details are intended to highlight the main idea. Some of the ways that supporting details may be organized include the following:

Analogy

An analogy is a relationship between two things or ideas. These may be similar to or different from one another. For instance, a person may say that oil is to water what fans of one sports team are to fans of another team. This analogy suggests that the fans of two separate sports teams are not going to mix with each other very well; this is similar to how oil and water do not mix properly.

Asking a Question

A question can be asked and then answered by the writer. The question is posed to help the reader recognize what is going to be discussed in the passage or article. For instance, a writer may ask the reader, "What is the most beautiful place in the world?" The reader is then given time to think about beautiful places. The writer will then talk about a specific place that relates to the main idea.

Cause and Effect

Cause and effect focuses on understanding why certain things happen. A person may talk about why a glass bottle breaks after someone drops it. The cause, in this case, involves why the bottle fell. The effect is the glass shattering. The cause directly impacts the effect.

Chronological Order

The main idea may be supported by a series of chronologically organized details. A passage may begin with a main idea, expanding on that sequentially over the next few sentences or paragraphs, and wrap up with a clear conclusion. The content's logical order helps readers to understand the general main idea.

Compare and Contrast

The main idea may be compared with something else. Two vehicles may be compared with each other, for instance. Engine features may be compared as well as wheels, stereo systems, and dashboards. Discussing how vehicles are similar or different to one another helps develop the main idea which might be which vehicle is better, for instance.

Generalization

Generalizing may involve anything related to the subject matter. It may be a summary of whatever is being discussed. Generalization may work best if enough factual or supporting information is provided. The summarization used here should be good enough to produce a detailed response that works accordingly based on certain information.

<u>Problem and Solution</u>
A writer may begin a passage by discussing a problem, lead readers through why the problem matters and then conclude the passage by providing details that support a particular solution.

Hypothesis

A hypothesis is a prediction based on related facts. The hypothesis requires further testing to confirm a predicted outcome, and sometimes the hypothesis may be proven incorrect. The writer may introduce the hypothesis at the start of a passage. The hypothesis may be referenced later and then highlighted once again at the end when the author lets readers know whether it was proven true or false.

You are most likely to find a hypothesis in a scientific report. The hypothesis must be based upon observations and research. It must be realistic and easy to test. The results of the test should be measured versus the hypothesis. Any cases where the hypothesis is proven wrong should be discussed at the end of a passage, along with details on why the prediction was incorrect.

Refutation

Refutation involves an opposing viewpoint that is brought up and then disputed. In this case, the writer might make an argument and then introduce an opposing claim. The opposing claim is discussed briefly and then challenged.

Spatial Order

Spatial order involves ideas being introduced in an order based on location. Items may be listed from left to right or from top to bottom or otherwise similarly arranged. Spatial order is used to illustrate what is on a map, diagram or other visual data representation. Some of the words students may notice in a spatial order report include above, behind, down, up, under and to the left or right. Sometimes the most important details in a spatially ordered passage are listed at the beginning based on how important the content is.

Keywords

Certain words may appear in passages more often than others. The keywords in a passage refer to the most important concepts an author is discussing. Being able to identify, define and apply those words is important to understanding the passage. Keywords can often be identified because they're repeated frequently, returned to over and over as an author makes an argument.

Meanings of Words and Phrases in Context

Every word will have a certain contextual meaning in a passage. One word may have an entirely different meaning depending on context. For example, "oversight" in one context can mean to overlook something. But in another context, the same word "oversight" means to supervise. It is therefore vital for a reader to understand words in context.

One way to identify a word or phrase in context is to look at the antonyms and synonyms in a passage. One passage may use multiple synonyms for a single word to place an emphasis on something. Noticing synonyms throughout the work can help a reader understand the feelings that the writer has toward a certain subject. Similarly, noticing how antonyms are used to contrast two items may help determine context.

Inferences or Implications

An implication is an indirect expression, such as a threat. For example, if someone in a passage vaguely says, while looking directly at a character, "Some people's jobs may be on the line," the implication is clearly that said character's job is in danger.

An inference involves noticing the implication. So if the character in question hears "Some people's jobs may be on the line," he or she will then infer that there's trouble coming. You infer something based on an implication. First someone implies, then you draw a conclusion—the inference.

To identify implications and inferences in text, look for context, chosen wording, adjectives, repeated words, any words that are highlighted (such as italicized), etc.

Fact or Opinion

A fact can be confirmed, measured or observed. This includes information that is backed up by the data that the writer is presenting. Sometimes this might come from personal research. It may also come from outside sources that are cited. Regardless of where the data comes from, the content should be something that a reader can identify or even duplicate.

An opinion is a belief that a person has. A writer may have formed his opinion based on what he has personally read or experienced, but the opinion remains strictly personal and is not based upon scientific research or clear-cut facts. Words like "probably," "feel," "I think" and "believe" are often signs that a writer is stating an opinion.

To decide if something in a passage is a fact or opinion:

- Look for any indications that a person has tried to confirm the information being presented, such as research studies.

- Look for emotional words (i.e., best or worst) which may indicate strong feelings rather than facts.

- Identify an author's experience. If a doctor is discussing a medical topic for example, that's more likely to be factual than if a layperson is discussing the same topic.

- Check any sources that are used. Legitimate sources like an academic journal or a study can be an indication that the work in question is reliable and factual. An opinion will usually not include any specific sources. Be careful to look at biases—sources that may appear factual but which are actually only being used to back up a personal belief.

Interpreting Information from Visual Data

Visual data can be a line graph, pie chart, table or an index, among other sources. A writer may use visuals to help readers understand data being used within the written text. You are more likely to find visual data in news reports and newspapers or periodicals, including academic journals. The visual data should be interpreted by:

1. **Reading the title of the visual data.** The title is listed at the top or bottom of an image such as a chart or table. The title clearly tells readers what will be contained in the chart, table, index, etc.

2. **Looking at any variables that are listed.** The variables may be listed in a small box to the side of a graphic. These may also be included in one column to the side of a larger chart or table. The variables explain what is measured in the graphic and are linked to the title.

3. **Noticing the proportions of a visual image and how certain values compare with each other.** For a chart, certain numbers or readings may dramatically stand out from others in the same chart. For a graph, a certain space may be higher or lower than other items. A pie chart may also include

one portion that takes up much more space than others. The data in the chart should be identified based on the most noticeable information and then compared with other variables listed.

Phonics

Words can be sounded out to help a student understand how they are pronounced. Phonics helps students read certain words in passages, particularly longer words or words that include more syllables. When students are using phonics, the following things should be kept in mind:

1. **Vowels.** Each vowel has its own sound. Vowels are a, e, i, o, u and sometimes y.

2. **Long and short vowels.** Each vowel has a short and a long sound. For example, the "a" in *cap* is short and the "a" in *cape* is long.

3. **Vowel combinations.** Vowel combinations may include ou, oo, ea, ie and ai. These combinations produce particular sounds.

4. **Consonant sounds.** Some consonants have two sounds. The "s" sound may be an "s" sound as in *sack* or a "z" sound as in *rise*. The "c" may have the sound of "k" as in *cat* or "s" as in *nice*.

5. **Consonant combinations.** Consonant combinations link two consonants to create a distinct sound, such as th, sh, ch, gh or ph as in the following: th as in *thing*, sh as in *ship*, ch as in *change*, gh as in *enough*, and ph as in *phone*.

Students are encouraged to sound out words based on the vowel and consonant sounds in each syllable. Also, students should be taught how the syllables are linked with each.

Breaking Words into Parts

Words can be organized by syllable so the reader or speaker can decipher the word. There are three things to notice when breaking words down:

1. **Root word.** The root word will have a certain standard definition that may be utilized on its own. For example, *love* can be a root word.

2. **Prefix.** The prefix appears at the beginning of a word. This is used to change the meaning of the word, in most cases, to change the word to a negative. Un-, in-, dis-, non- or un- may be added to the beginning of a word to indicate the opposite of the root word, such as unloved (note the addition to the root word *love)*, inactive, disjointed and nonpayment.

3. **Suffix.** The suffix appears at the end of a root word. Suffixes include: -ing, -ion, -ant, -ment, and -ation and many more. Using the root word *love* once more, you could add a suffix such as -*ing* to create the word *loving*.

Compound Words

Compound words are words that feature two single words that are joined. This often entails two words that each have one or two syllables. By adding the two words together, a new word is formed. "Water" and "melon" both have specific meanings, for instance. But they can be combined to create the compound word "watermelon," which in itself has a distinct meaning.

Syllables

Syllables are sound units that combine with one another to produce a full word. A syllable can be recognized by vowel sounds. For example, in-hab-it has three vowel sounds and three syllables; in-hab-it-ing has four vowel sounds and four syllables. A student will have an easier time identifying what a word means or how it is said by taking all the syllables and combining them together. The syllables may also help identify any suffixes or prefixes while helping the reader identify the root word. For instance, the letters "tt" may be found together in one word. The word "committed" is an example of this. By reviewing the syllables, the student can pronounce this as com-mit-ted.

Synonyms, Antonyms and Homonyms

Synonyms are words that have similar meanings. For instance, a person may use the word "small" and the synonym "little." Or "wet" is a synonym of "damp." The words can be used in the same passage to create interest. The key is to avoid unnecessary repetition which could bore a reader.

Antonyms are words that have opposite meanings. The word "large" would be an antonym of "small." "Dry" would be an antonym of "wet." Antonyms are used to compare ideas or concepts.

A homonym is a word that sounds like another, but the two words have different meanings. "Way" and "weigh," "ate" and "eight," "rain" and "reign" are examples. The two words may be pronounced in exactly or nearly the same way.

Alphabetizing Words

Alphabetizing involves putting words in order according to the alphabet. If words begin with the same letter, the second letter is considered. For example, plum, punt, pear, point, pass, in alphabetical order would be listed as "pass, pear, plum, point and punt."

Three Stages to Teach the Alphabet

You may introduce students to the alphabet in three stages. First, introduce the letter in a "this is" period. The student will see the letters for the first time and recognize them. The phonetic sound of the letter should be introduced.

The second stage is a "show me" period. The student may be told to take a series of papers that feature the letters and say the letters on each paper. You may ask the student to point to the "b." After this, you may test how well the student can identify the "c" that comes after "b," and so on.

The third stage is a "what is this" that involves the student being asked to write the letter and sound it out. The student should recall the proper order of the letters in the alphabet at this point.

Helping Students Use Reading Strategies

Various strategies may be used before, during or after a student reads a passage. Not all of the strategies listed here can be used in a single passage. They should be used based on whatever a reader might be most comfortable using.

Flyover

A flyover in reading is where the reader looks at a passage for a brief time. The key is to identify the most important content so the reader has a basic idea of what the passage is about. The reader should notice the keywords used in the passage, definitions or ideas introduced. The specific details should not be considered too much. Those details can be covered in a later in-depth reading. The practice is particularly used in cases where a reader requires extra time to understand the concepts being introduced in a passage.

Skimming

Skimming focuses on only looking for the main idea of a work and figuring out what theme is found throughout the passage. By finding the main idea, the reader will understand what to expect when reading the passage completely later on. The process may take about as much time as a flyover.

Skimming allows the reader to recognize how the first sentence of each paragraph leads to the next sentence or paragraph. The main idea gleaned in the skimming process will move the act of reading forward. After reading the first sentence, the student will look for data that relates to the main idea while using that first sentence as a baseline. The student will be less likely to be confused about the paragraph as it is being read.

Skimming works best when reading informational or nonfiction works but can be used for fictional works as well. The skimming process may help readers to get a quick preview of actions or events in a passage. The student should review each fictional paragraph carefully to ensure the time frame is accurate and that the events link to each other. Skimming may also help readers quickly identify relationships between characters, including how characters may respond to other characters or events.

Scanning

Scanning is very different from skimming. Where skimming involves looking for the main idea, scanning involves finding specific content. The reader must look for a certain keyword, description or other content. Part of this includes looking for specific words or ideas that may lead to a very specific piece of information. Scanning works best for nonfiction passages when a student is aiming to find the essence of a piece of writing. This may be utilized in fictional work in cases where a student wishes to find information on a subject of value.

An example of scanning is reading a book to find certain information, but not reading the entire passage. For example, say you want to find information on how long a giraffe's neck may be. Therefore, you scan the entry to find keywords like "length" or "height," which will direct you to the information you seek. There may be plenty of other interesting information about giraffes in the passage, but your goal when scanning is just to hone in on the information you're looking for. When students are answering multiple choice questions and have limited time on a test, a good strategy to teach is to read the questions first, then scan the passage to find keywords that lead to the answers.

Tentative Summary

A tentative summary is produced after a flyover or other brief reading of the material. The summary entails the reader determining the most important parts of the work and then producing a brief summary. The summary is especially helpful when a person is trying to eliminate choices in a test.

The student may keep notes on the details of a piece of work to create a summary. This could be useful for gauging a student's expectations of a work. The practice may also help identify how well the student can predict or analyze the content.

Opening and Closing Sentences In a Paragraph

The opening and closing sentences are often the most important ones to review in a paragraph. The opening sentence introduces the idea to be discussed in the paragraph. This may include a specific definition. The closing sentence may be a summary or conclusion of whatever was discussed.

Signal Words

Signal words are likely to be found at the start of a paragraph or at least near the beginning. You may find information in each signal word on what an author is trying to prove, the order of something or any practices used to compare items. Words like "first," "second," "next" or "finally" may be used to let the reader know where signal words are within a passage. Other words like "both," "likewise" or "similarly" may be used to state that two items being discussed and are similar to each other. Other words like "in contrast" or "on the other hand" may express that the writer is going to talk about the differences between certain concepts or ideas.

Some signal words focus on the cause and effect relationships between items. The words "for this reason" or "as a result" are used to explain that a certain result will occur due to a specific event or other action. Words like "due to" or "because of" may also focus on discussing what causes certain actions to occur.

Understanding the Author's Intention

Every writer has a certain attitude or intention toward whatever they have written. A student can be asked to identify why an author wrote a certain passage or what that person was trying to say. The angle that the author is trying to focus on may also be a factor. The reader may be asked to find the most important detail in the passage that indicates the feelings that the writer had.

A reader may also consider the author's experience and background involving the subject matter. For instance, the writer of a paper on biology might have a master's degree in biology and have held a job in the field for years. That person is likely to understand the science field and could be a more authoritative, factual figure. Any experiences that the person had in the field should also be noted.

Emotional Words

Some words indicate emotion and are used to illustrate what the writer really thinks or feels about a subject. A writer may use adjectives to illustrate their interest, preference or fear. Negative adjectives may suggest that the writer does not have positive feelings about what they are writing about. The wording could suggest a sense of bias in the work.

The student must consider the positive or negative nature of the words being used. For purposes of understanding, a reader can organize the words based on what is the most positive content versus the most negative.

In a first person narrative, the emotional words typically relate to what the writer is thinking or feeling.

<u>Building Anticipation for the Content</u>

You can help students become interested in the content you are teaching by having them learn about what they will discuss in a text. Anticipation entails a preview or review of a text's themes. Copies of a guide may be provided to students to help them gain interest in the subject matter. Students can discuss the content with you and then review the things they discover in the content based on what they were anticipating.

Don't give away too many details at this point. However, you can encourage your students to scan or skim a text to see what the main ideas of the work may be. As the students read, they will start to notice some of the themes or topics you might have introduced. The goal is to preview the content without adding more details than necessary. This is to allow students themselves to explore the subject matter and to see what they can find in the work.

Asking Questions to Gauge Understanding

You may ask a student various questions to determine what that student does or does not understand in a passage. You may ask the student to paraphrase the passage, for instance. The goal is to encourage the reader to understand whatever is being discussed in the work in question. You may ask the student the following questions, among many others:

- What specific terms in the passage were most important? This includes a look at certain keywords, definitions, facts and opinions that were posed.

- How does the content in the passage link to other information in the work? This may entail reviewing how one detail connects to another in the next paragraph or chapter.

- Are there facts provided in the passage? List the facts versus any opinions found in a text.

- What information does the writer put greater emphasis on? You may notice this based on the attention given to concepts or ideas within the work.

Reading an Index

An index is a feature at the back of a book that lists information on topics discussed in the book. The index will include details on the subjects and the pages where that content can be found. The content can also help a reader to preview the subject matter within the book, thus producing a better idea of the main point an author wishes to illustrate.

When reading an index, the topics or items will be listed in alphabetical order. A person's name will be listed with the last name first. The item is then followed by a page number or multiple numbers. Sometimes the pages are listed in consecutive order (154-157); in other cases, the content is found on many pages (154, 157, 188, 205). A combination of the pages may be listed (154-157, 188).

An entry in an index may have several subtopics. For instance, an index may list North Carolina as a topic. You may find that the city of Raleigh is mentioned on pages 35 and 48, and the city of Charlotte is on page 54. The geology of the state is mentioned from pages 25 to 28. Since there are many aspects of the state to talk about, it's logical to include several subtopics in the index.

A "See also" section may be included in an index. This tells a person to go to a certain part of the index to find more information. For example, an index entry may be, "Hurricanes, 45-56. See also tropical systems." While you will find information on hurricanes from pages 45 to 56, you can get more information on them by reviewing the tropical systems section of the index.

For entries where the content is listed on many pages, the first page listed is often an introduction to the topic. For example, you might see an entry that says "Biometrics, 35, 38, 42-43, 46." You can turn to page 35 to see the first details on biometrics. You may find information on the definition of biometrics or how it relates to the subject matter.

Assessing a Student's Ability to Understand the Text

A student can be asked about the main idea of a text or about very specific things that were listed in the text. The answers given by the student may indicate understanding.

The student may not necessarily interpret the content in the same way that you do though. Be aware of this when talking with the student about the subject matter.

Using a Dictionary

A dictionary may be used when reviewing words that a student might not be familiar with. The dictionary will give the meaning (or meanings, if the word has more than one), the pronunciation and possible synonyms or antonyms. The student will also see how a word may be used as a noun or verb and will be provided with examples of the word used in a sentence. The verb tenses may also be listed.

The student should be asked which definition of the word best fits how the word is used in the writing. For instance, a word like "challenge" may be used as either a noun to suggest that something is difficult, as in "a challenge was given to the student," or as a verb where someone is performing an action, as in "he challenged the professor." The reader should look at the definitions and context to determine how the word is used. Some words may include three or more definitions.

You may also come across singular and plural forms, as well as cases where the word is an adverb. The spelling of the base word may vary based on how that word operates within a sentence. When tenses are not listed, basic spelling or grammatical rules may be utilized.

Interpreting Written Directions

A teacher may give certain directions that a student must follow when identifying how an assignment is to be completed or how a task is to be finished. Students should be taught to watch for words such as "first," "next," etc.

In addition to sequential transition words, the student must be aware of how the steps are connected to each other. This includes looking at whether certain actions may be directly related to earlier events. For instance, one step in a guide on how to bake cookies will state, "Add two eggs and two cups of milk." The next step will be, "Stir the ingredients together." The student should recognize these directions are directly linked to one another in a kind of cause and effect.

<u>Statements that Agree or Disagree</u>

Another way of analyzing comprehension is to have students produce agree/disagree answers about certain parts of a text. The students are asked to agree or disagree about certain statements before they read the text in question. After reading the text, students will see if their opinions changed. Students can be encouraged to provide textual evidence for why their opinions did or did not change, citing page numbers and passages, for instance.

The agree/disagree statements may be used for most types of readings including both fiction and nonfiction. This strategy works best in situations where the student is not familiar with the subject matter.

Notes on the Testing Process

The reading segment of the test will focus both on reading comprehension and reading skills. You'll find passages of varying lengths and will need to answer questions about their content.

In other cases, you will focus on different points relating to the process of reading. This includes looking at how words are ordered, how phrases and sentences are constructed, punctuation and the rules for grammar.

Reading Questions
Questions 1-4 are for the following passage:

Although the United States Football League would not be formed until 1982, the concept of the USFL was first brought up in the mid-1960s. David Dixon, a businessman who supported the New Orleans Saints and the construction of the Louisiana Superdome, felt that a professional football league that played its games in the spring and summer would be a viable endeavor.

As Dixon looked at some of the National Football League's competitors and how those leagues failed, he noticed many trends. He found that many of those leagues did not get the television contracts that they required early on in their existence. He also found that it was often difficult to find owners that were willing to lose money for a few years before they could turn a profit.

After a while, Dixon was able to find many owners that could start teams, a television broadcasting contract and various venues that the league could host. However, there were some problems where teams were refused access to certain stadiums. There were also plans to try and add a few teams from Canada to the league, but the Canadian government was threatening to pass legislation that would prevent American football leagues from competing in the country. The problems were difficult at the start, but they weren't as bad as those that would eventually lead to the league's downfall in 1986.

1. David Dixon felt that the idea of playing football games in the spring or summer was:
    a. Risky
    b. Dangerous
    c. Profitable
    d. Developmental
2. What is the main concept of the second paragraph?
    a. Looking at other leagues
    b. Thinking about locations
    c. Planning insurance for the league
    d. Seeing how to create a new NFL team
3. The Canadian government was _____ about the idea of an American football league competing in Canada:
    a. Excited
    b. Frustrated
    c. Curious
    d. Neutral
4. The overall purpose of the passage is to explain how a professional football league was:
    a. Formed
    b. Dissolved
    c. Expanded
    d. Operated

Question 5 entails the following sentence:

The government should try and find a way to resolve the school lunch dispute.

5. The main idea of the sentence is that:
    a. There is a school lunch issue
    b. The government works for students
    c. The government should take action
    d. Schools are in trouble

6. An analogy requires the following words in a sentence:
    a. Is as
    b. About
    c. Sort of
    d. Generally

Question 7 entails the following sentence:

The backyard was flooded and had to be drained with an outside pump. The hurricane that crossed through the area really took its toll.

7. In this sentence, what are the cause and effect?
    a. The hurricane caused a need to get an outside pump
    b. The flooding caused the house to get a pump
    c. The hurricane caused the flooding
    d. All of the above

Question 8 entails the following passage:

An interesting fact about Interstate 40 is that the highway includes unique markers at its starting and ending points. There is one sign to the west in Barstow, California, and another sign in Wilmington, North Carolina. Each sign lets the reader know how many miles there are between the two ends of Interstate 40.

8. What is the main idea of the passage?

    a. Interstate 40 is a very long highway.

    b. There are distinct markers on the two ends of Interstate 40.

    c. Interstate 40 goes from California to North Carolina.

    d. It takes a while to travel Interstate 40.

Question 9 entails the following passage:

Joseph was often frustrated with trying to find a good parking space. He noticed that many people who have electric vehicles were given access to premium parking spaces that were more appealing. But Joseph didn't have the money to get a new electric vehicle. He figured that he had to get to the parking lot earlier in the day to try and get a better spot.

9. What is the main idea of the passage?

    a. Joseph looked at the electric cars.

    b. Joseph struggled with getting up early.

    c. Joseph couldn't find a good parking spot.

    d. Joseph had to find a way to get a better parking spot.

Questions 10 and 11 focus on the following two sentences:

The teacher wanted to discuss the upcoming class assignment with her students. The students were not all that excited about it though.

    10. In the first sentence, "discuss" means:

        a. Grade

        b. Plan

        c. Schedule

        d. Talk about

    11. The students were not excited because:

        a. They were in school instead of outside

        b. They were bored

        c. There was a new assignment to work on

        d. The teacher wasn't interesting

Question 12 covers the sentence:

The baseball team was enthusiastic about winning the championship.

12. Enthusiastic in this sentence means:

    a. Happy

    b. Worried

    c. Sad

    d. Confused

13. A tentative summary may be utilized to:

    a. Look at what the main idea of a passage may be

    b. Determine the motive of the writer

    c. Identify specific terms in a passage

    d. Find information on characters in a passage

Questions 14-16 involve the following passage:

The Chicago elevated rail service, or the L as it is also called, provides people in Chicago with regular train services to and from various places in and around Chicago. The system offers eight lines, with each line designated by color.

The lines on the elevated rail service include the Red Line, a line that moves toward both Wrigley Field and Guaranteed Rate Field, the homes of the Chicago Cubs and White Sox baseball teams. The Blue Line goes to O'Hare airport, while the Orange Line heads to Midway airport. Other lines include the Brown, Green, Purple, Pink and Yellow.

Many of the lines move into the central part of Chicago or the Loop. Various lines meet with one another at the Loop. People can transfer from one line to the next here. Some of the stations around the Loop are also underground stations that have exits leading to the city streets.

A few cities outside of Chicago are served by the L. You can visit Rosemont on the Blue Line, Evanston and Northwestern University on the Purple Line, Oak Park on the Brown Line and Skokie on the Yellow Line.

14. All of these are the names of lines on the Chicago elevated rail system except:

    a. Pink

    b. Green

    c. Silver

    d. Yellow

15. A baseball fan would be more interested in this line:

    a. Green

    b. Orange

    c. Red

    d. Purple

16. In the third paragraph, the Loop refers to:

    a. A busy part of Chicago

    b. An outside part of Chicago

    c. A wide-open area

    d. A major rail station

Question 17 involves the following sentence:

The first thing to notice about the bill is its budget.

17. Which of these words in the sentence can be used as a signal word?

    a. First

    b. Thing

    c. Bill

    d. Budget

Question 18 entails the following sentence:

The submarine is very large in size.

18. Can this be interpreted as a fact or opinion?

    a. Fact

    b. Opinion

    c. Neither

    d. Both

19. A closing sentence in a paragraph is designed to:

    a. Convey the main idea

    b. Summarize the paragraph

    c. Add new details

    d. Produce a transition

20. A signal word relating to something that caused an event would be:

    a. Because of

    b. Likewise

    c. Finally

    d. Before

Answers

1. c. The passage states that Dixon felt that the idea of playing games in the summer or spring would be intriguing and that there was a demand for it. Therefore, he saw his efforts as being potentially profitable.
2. a. The main idea of the paragraph is that Dixon was looking around to see what caused other leagues that failed in the past to struggle. This was to keep his new league from failing.
3. b. The Canadian government was willing to pass a bill outlawing the American league from operating in Canada. Therefore, the government could be interpreted as being frustrated over the idea of the league playing.
4. a. The passage focuses on how the football league was formed and how Dixon worked to develop the league over the course of many years.
5. c. The word "should" shows that the writer is trying to persuade the reader to see that the government needs to do something about school lunches.
6. a. The analogy is designed to illustrate a relationship between two items. An example would be, "The football team is as strong as the hockey team is as fast."
7. d. The cause and effect can be noted by looking at an event that took place after an initial event. There must be a strong relationship between the events in question. In this example, each of the possible answers shows a connection—the hurricane comes through, the backyard is flooded, a pump comes in to correct the issue.

8. b. While all of the answers are factual, the main idea of the passage is that Interstate 40 has distinct signs on its two ends to show people where the road goes.
9. d. The entire paragraph focuses on Joseph thinking about what he can do to get a better parking spot.
10. d. To discuss something is to talk about the concept with other people.
11. c. The students in the sentence are responding to the teacher talking about the new assignment.
12. a. Enthusiasm is a feeling that a person might experience when one is happy about something happening. In this case, the baseball team is happy about winning a major championship.
13. a. The tentative summary helps to figure out what one might do in a test. This includes looking at the main idea as it is highlighted through certain keywords. The process is used with nonfictional work in most cases, although it may work for fictional content.
14. c. Silver is not one of the colors mentioned in the passage.
15. c. The passage states that the Red Line goes to both of the city's major ballparks. Therefore, a baseball fan would be more interested in the Red Line than the others.
16. a. The Loop is a name for a very busy part of Chicago that is in the middle of the city where many people visit for business or tourism. The Loop is therefore a very busy part of the city that has many rail stations that are shared among multiple lines.
17. a. *First* is the signal word as the word lets the reader know that the budget is the first thing for people to

notice about the bill. The reader now knows that there is an ordinal series of details to follow.
18. b. The statement could be factual, but there is no evidence cited that the submarine is indeed large. Therefore, the statement is an opinion. The content would become a fact if the statement had specific information pertaining to the size of the submarine such as weight or length.
19. b. Whereas the first sentence in a paragraph often introduces what the paragraph will be about, the last sentence will summarize the points made in text. The summary is related to the main idea, but it is not exactly the main idea. Rather, the last sentence establishes a vital point on the main idea.
20. a. "Because of" states that something is happening due to a prior event taking place. There is a direct link between the event in question and the action that occurred.

Section 2: Writing

The writing segment of the ParaPro test focuses on understanding how words are organized, using words grammatically correctly and using words to formulate concepts that are easy to understand. The goal is to help students write logically and coherently.

What You Will Be Tested On

1. You will be tested on many factors relating to how writing tasks are to be completed. This includes an emphasis on any grammatical errors. Any errors in word usage, spelling, the various parts of speech and punctuation may also be covered.

You will also be tested on how to assist students in understanding what they can do when working on various writing tasks. Some of this involves helping students to plan their writing project including outlining, determining an audience, etc.

Parts of Speech

Noun

This is a word that refers to a person, place, thing or concept. A person can be referenced either directly through one's name or professional status (a proper noun indicated by a capital letter, such as John, Mary, Mr., Dr., California). A noun may include anything directly seen, noticed or felt. For a concept, the noun would refer to a value or feeling—happiness, sadness, anger and pride.

A proper noun refers to a very specific entity or concept. For instance, a supermarket would be a common noun. A name for a specific supermarket like Publix, Harris Teeter or Safeway is a proper noun because a certain brand name is being utilized. A person's name is a proper noun, such as Mary, John, Mrs. Smith, Dr. Jones. A more generic reference to a person referring to one's profession, appearance or anything other than a name is a common noun, such as a pharmacist, teacher or librarian

Verb

A verb is a word that denotes action. This may also include what a subject is doing. The action that one participates in is a verb, such as learns, learned, see or saw. An intransitive verb has the word 'to' in front of it, such as to eat, to swim, to learn.

A verb may be in a present, past or future tense, such as eat, ate, have eaten, will eat; or play, played, had played, will play. A verb may be in a singular or plural form to reflect whether the verb is impacting only one person or many people at a time. For example, I write or he writes, they or we write; I wrote, he wrote, he has written, they wrote, they have written, we wrote, we have written. This is called verb conjugation. There are specific rules for certain types of verbs and some irregular verbs that don't follow the rules, such as I catch, you catch, he catches, we catch, they catch; or I see, I saw, I have seen, etc.

Adjective

An adjective describes (modifies) a noun or pronoun. For instance, a cat may be hungry, sleepy or playful. Those three words can be used as adjectives if they are placed before the noun—"the hungry cat," "the sleepy cat."

Superlatives are also adjectives, such as heaviest, heavier, smaller, smallest, older, oldest.

Adverb

An adverb modifies a verb or adjective. This word is how a certain action is completed. In many cases, the adverb will have "-ly" added to the end of the word. In the sentence "The driver suddenly changed lanes," *suddenly* is the adverb because it modifies the verb "changed." An adverb can also modify another adverb. In the sentence "The driver can change lanes very suddenly," *very* would be used as the adverb that modifies suddenly. An adverb may also be found at the beginning of a sentence. "Suddenly, the driver changed lanes" is an example of this.

An adverb may tell the reader one of four things relating to the verb:

1. **When** – The adverb lets the person know that there is a time for the action. Some of these adverbs include after, before, today, tomorrow, yesterday, since and soon.

2. **Where** – An adverb may also explain where something is taking place. Adverbs, in this case, include below, above, far, near, outside, inside and there.

3. **How** – These adverbs refer to an emotion or feeling that accompanies the verb. Some examples are calmly, sadly, quietly, loudly, knowingly and quickly. An example would be, "The player slowly tried to field the baseball." While the adverb "slowly" could be eliminated, that adverb is being used to explain

that the baseball player was unsuccessful in his attempt to field a baseball. The adverb changes the action that takes place and adds to the description of the action.

4. **Frequency** – These adverbs explain the frequency of an action. These adverbs include usually, never, always, once, often, frequently and seldom. For example, in the sentence "The chef rarely uses garlic," *rarely* indicates time.

Pronoun

A pronoun replaces a noun. The noun may be a personal or possessive pronoun.

Personal: A personal pronoun will stand in for the main subject matter. For instance, a personal pronoun can be I, you, he, she, it, we or they. A personal pronoun may also be used for an object. Some of the personal pronouns include me, you, him, her, it, us or them. In the sentence "The mechanic fixed the car for me," *me* is the object of the sentence.

Possessive: A possessive pronoun indicates ownership. The pronoun is used as an adjective or can stand on its own. A pronoun that is an adjective is most often placed before a noun, such as my, our, his, her, its, their or your. Other possessive pronouns appear after a verb, such as mine, yours, ours, his, hers or theirs.

All pronouns must match the gender being used. If a pronoun is used to refer to a female subject, words such as she or hers, he or his must be used to indicate gender. Plural pronouns like ours and theirs do not indicate gender.

A gender-neutral pronoun, such as *its*, is used to indicate possession of a thing, not a person or place.

Preposition

A preposition indicates a relationship to a certain item. Some prepositions include about, at, for, before, like, of, on, to, in or with.

Conjunctions

A conjunction links two parts of a sentence. The word "and" is the most common conjunction. Other conjunctions are but, or, when, because and so.

Some conjunctions may be paired. If/then is one such example. The sentence "If he ate dinner, then he is no longer hungry" is an example of this. Other pairs include either/or, both/and, only/but and also.

Interjections

An interjection is a word that produces an emotional response or indicates a strong emphasis. In many cases, the interjection will include an exclamation point at the end to emphasize an emotional response. For instance, a sentence may include "Wow! The driver is going fast." The word "Wow!" is being used as the interjection.

An interjection may be used in cases where the writer wants to place a strong emphasis on something that happened. An example here is "Great! The football team won the championship." The "great" interjection is used to add importance to the event. It's typically a big deal for a football team or any other sports team to win a championship. An interjection is not necessary for a minor event like going to the supermarket or paying a bill.

The Use of Clauses

Independent and Dependent Clauses

An independent clause is another word for a sentence. You may find a sentence that features more than one independent clause. A dependent clause is not fully complete. An example is "In spite of the effort, the driver was unable to avoid the rush hour traffic." This is a complete sentence where the dependent clause at the beginning links to the independent clause.

Adverb Clauses

An adverb clause starts with a subordinating conjunction such as although, because, until, when or any other qualifier. The adverb clause is designed to answer a question. An example is "We traveled to the city because we wanted to visit the fair;" *because* is the conjunction that supports the adverb clause.

Adjective Clause

An adjective clause is also called a relative clause. The clause will modify the noun or pronoun. An example would be the sentence "We enjoyed the festival, which was one that occurs yearly." The clause "which was one that occurs yearly" modifies festival.

Simple and Complex Sentences

A simple sentence has one verb. An example is "The car dealer has three vehicles." The sentence will become a complex sentence when a dependent clause is added. In this case, the example will expand to "The car dealer has three vehicles from multiple car manufacturers." The content that was added at the end is a dependent clause.

A complex-compound sentence may also be formed when one dependent clause is accentuated with at least two independent clauses. An example is: "Because the car dealer wants to offer more choices to customers, it has three different car manufacturers that have vehicles available at the dealership, thus letting people know what is available." The first part that entails the car dealer wanting to offer choices is the dependent clause. The other two parts that are separated by the commas are the independent clauses that can stand apart on their own.

The goal of any sentence or passage is clarity. In the above example, the part "thus helping get people to see what is available" can be rewritten as "The dealer is helping people to see what is available." This helps shorten the sentence and clarify key details.

Subject and Predicate

The subject is the noun that performs the action. The subject (a common or proper noun) is a person, place or thing. The predicate is the action that the subject completes. The predicate may also be an assertion relating to the original subject.

In the sentence, "Jeff went to the shopping mall," *Jeff* is the subject. He is the one who is going to the shopping mall. The predicate entails how he went to the shopping mall. This is the action that Jeff is completing. The phrase "went to the shopping mall" may be used as the complete predicate, while "went" could be a simple predicate as it includes the basic verb of Jeff having gone someplace.

Using the complete predicate is often recommended in cases where the action being discussed is foreign and has not been introduced yet. The simple predicate may be used when the action has occurred many times over. The simple variant may also work if the complete predicate is too long.

The subject may be used as a common or proper noun. A pronoun may also be used to replace the noun. The predicate contains at least one verb and is the action that the subject completes. A series of nouns, such as the names of two separate people or a descriptor of a person ("the man with the green shirt") can also be the subject of the sentence. The main verb will be the simple predicate with the adjectives, adverbs or other accompanying information being used as the complete predicate. The complete predicate can include as many of these as needed, although it could be written without an adjective or adverb if needed.

Grammar

Grammar refers to the rules governing how sentences are written. The following section focuses on the most common grammatical rules.

Subject-Verb Agreement

The subject and verb in a sentence must be in the same tense or of the same number. This includes both items being singular or plural in nature. For instance, "The kids skate" is an example of proper agreement as the subject and verb are plural.

Verb Tense

All verbs must have the same tense within the same sentence. When multiple actions occur in the same sentence or within the same paragraph, the verbs must have the same tense: past, present or future tense. A correct example is "John bought the groceries while Mary cleaned the car." *Bought* and *cleaned* are both in the past tense as these events took place at the same time. "John buys the groceries while Mary cleaned the car" is incorrect as John's action is in the present while Mary's action is in the past.

Noun-Pronoun Agreement

Nouns and pronouns must agree with each other according to number and gender. The words must be singular or plural. For example, if the subject in a sentence is singular, the pronoun must be singular as in "John ran and he won the race." If the subject is feminine, the pronoun must also be feminine as in "Mary ran and she won the race."

Parallelism

Parallelism involves all the items in a sentence being in agreement in terms of grammatical form. Parallelism reduces the number of words in a sentence. The practice keeps the sentence from being too complicated and avoids run-on sentences. For example, "Michelle likes to watch television each night and she also relaxes by eating pizza." The structure becomes parallel by combining ideas as in "Michelle spends each night relaxing by watching television and eating pizza."

Agreement

Some people use indefinite pronouns incorrectly. An indefinite pronoun such as anyone, everyone, each, either or neither should be interpreted as a singular pronoun. Therefore, a singular verb is to be used. Example of this include "Anyone can try," "Everyone is welcome," "Each person can drive a car" or "Neither person can drive a truck." The pronoun will match the verb in any of these cases.

Some indefinite pronouns may also be singular or plural in form. These include pronouns such as all, any, none or some. The pronoun must match a verb that is singular or plural depending on the reference. An instance of this is "All people are ready" or "All the money is available." Another example would be "Some of the people are ready to work" or "Some person might be present for work."

Referring to an Institution

A larger institution that has many people involved is referenced by plural pronouns. A government, for example, is referred to by the pronoun *it*.

For example, "The government passed a bill," would become "*It* passed a bill" so long as it's clear from the paragraph's context that it's the government that the pronoun is being referred to.

Gerunds

A gerund is a verb that ends in '-ing' with that verb being used as a noun. The gerund may be used on its own as in "Swimming is good exercise." (swimming as a noun) or within a phrase as in "John enjoys his time swimming at the pool." (swimming as a verb). A possessive pronoun may be used before the gerund. For instance, 'running' is a gerund in "Running is important for your health." The word *running* can be both a verb and a noun.

Word Usage

Word usage involves words being used incorrectly. In most cases, this is due to a word being a homonym. A homonym is a word that sounds like another, but has a different meaning. There may also be cases where a word looks similar to another and a writer accidentally uses the wrong spelling.

A correct sentence would be "The author knows better than to write incorrectly." An incorrect sentence is "The author knows better then to write incorrectly." "Than" should be used here.

In some instances, changing a single letter will change the meaning of whatever someone is writing. This includes when a person changes "desert" to "dessert" by adding one more letter than needed and changes the meaning entirely.

Adding Verbs to Introduce Content

Some of the more common verbs that introduce content include described, asked, added, compared, acknowledged, remarked and offered. An example would be, "The student asked about the biology project." The verb in this sentence focuses on the student initiating the discussion on the biology project. Students should use an assortment of these verbs to avoid repetition in their writing.

Simple and Phrasal Verbs

A simple verb is one word and is direct. A phrasal verb includes more words. For example, "look out for" is a phrasal verb and can be shortened to "identify."

A phrasal verb often is a verb with a preposition or adverb. "Look into," "get better" and "back something up" are all examples of phrasal verbs. Each is identifiable by the verb having additional words. The content may be too vague and can be shortened for effect.

Point of View

Point of view is the specific perspective a passage is being written from.

First Person

The first person narrative focuses on a person directly telling a story. The narrative will involve the use of pronouns that relate to the self, such as I, me, we and us. A first person story may involve the narrator talking directly to the reader.

Second Person

The second person narrative involves the writer directly acknowledging the reader. The pronoun "you" and other related pronouns are used. An example of this may be in an argumentative essay when the writer is explaining something to the reader. It can also be used in giving instructions, particularly how-to guides.

Third Person

The third person format entails the writer being removed from the subject matter or narrative. The key is to keep the content from being influenced by personal opinions. Pronouns such as he, she, they, it, them, they and other relevant words are used.

Use of Commas

A comma is designed to separate parts of a sentence. An example is "Janet went to the store, but she did not get milk."

Clauses and Conjunctions

A comma is most often used between two clauses that are linked by certain conjunction such as but, and, or, so, for and nor.

No commas should be used when there are no conjunctions used between two independent clauses. A semicolon is used instead. An example here is "The family wanted to go; however, the market was closed." The semicolon may be used before such words as however, accordingly, still, consequently, also, thus and similarly. This may also go before groupings of words, such as on the other hand, for example, for instance and in addition.

Introductory Phrases

A comma can be used following an introductory phrase. For instance, a sentence may read "After the game began, the fans sat in their seats." The comma separates the introductory phrase from the main point of the sentence. You may also move the introductory part of the sentence to the end if you do not wish to use a comma; in the example above, you would write "The fans sat in their seats after the game began."

Adverbs

A comma should be used when there is a conjunctive adverb within the sentence. An example of this would be "The teacher, however, wanted the students to complete their tasks on time." Another example would be "However, the teacher wanted the students to finish their work on time."

A conjunctive adverb may be added where the emphasis is to be applied within the work. "However" is useful in cases where the reader needs to be informed that something is different and requires attention. "Besides" indicates there is a need to confirm some information. The key for all conjunctive adverbs is to use a comma to separate the adverb from the rest of the sentence.

Separating Items

Commas are used to separate items in a sentence. An example would be "The airport offers daily flights to Chicago, Atlanta, Houston, Toronto and Las Vegas."

Adding Non-Essential Data

Commas are used before and after you add extraneous information to a sentence. You may write a sentence such as "The car, a blue Toyota, moved down the road." The commas are used around the part that could be eliminated and the remaining words still constitute a sentence.

Comma Splice Error

A comma splice occurs when a comma is added where a period should be included. For instance, a splice will occur in "'I was very tired,' he said, 'what happened?'" The second comma in that example should be a period instead. The person who was speaking used two separate sentences. The second comma could be used if there was a continuation of the sentence: "'I was very tired,' he said, 'so I do not know what happened.'"

Use of a Semicolon

The semicolon separates two clauses that are linked to each other based on their subject matter. This may be used to link clauses in lieu of a comma. An author may write "Max drove to the supermarket; he could not find any bread." That sentence has two independent clauses and each can stand alone as separate sentences. Since these two clauses are so close to one another based on the subject matter, a semicolon may be used instead of a period.

Use of the Apostrophe

The apostrophe is a punctuation mark that may indicate possession or a contraction.

Possession

The apostrophe illustrates that a person possesses a certain item. For a singular noun, an apostrophe shows possession as in "Jane's car." An apostrophe is used in cases where the singular noun ends in an "s" as in "Charles' car."

Plural Possessives

Plural possessives may need an apostrophe as well, although this varies based on whether or not the noun ends in an "s." An example would be "the boys' toy." This means that many boys own a toy. The phrase "the boy's toy" means that only one boy owns the toy.

An apostrophe should not be added to any noun that is not possessive. When saying that people in the Jones family went to an event, you can write "The Joneses attended the event." You should not use an apostrophe in a form like "the Jones' or Jones's" unless the Jones family owns something.

The last letter of a word is always key when looking at a plural possession. A word that ends in -s, referring to two or more people, may include an -es, as in the "Charleses" or "Davises." A word that ends with an x or v may include -es, such as the "Knoxes."

Possessive Personal Pronouns

You may come across some apostrophe errors when using possessive personal pronouns. An apostrophe should not be added to a possessive pronoun. For instance, a passage should say "this is hers" and not "this is her's."

Contractions

Contractions shorten words. For example, "it is" is contracted to "it's"; "there is" becomes "there's" ; "do not" becomes "don't" ; I am becomes I'm, etc.

Be cautious when looking at how it's and its are used. 'Its' signifies ownership of something. "It's" is the contraction of "it is." Misused apostrophes are some of the most common punctuation mistakes.

The Rules of Spelling

A word may have two or more meanings depending on the correct spelling. For example, here and here, there and their, rain and reign. Generally, words follow certain rules of phonetics but there are many exceptions that have to be memorized.

Plural Forms

In some cases, a plural word will include -s or -es at the end. In other cases, you will have to change a few of the letters to create the plural form. For instance, *leaf* will become *leaves* in its plural form.

Homonyms

Homonyms are words that sound the same (homonyms) but are spelled differently. For instance, principle and principal, stationary and stationery.

Suffixes

A suffix, added to the end of a word, may change the spelling. A silent e may or may not be included before -ly. The word "time" can be expanded into "timely" with a silent e included. "Change" becomes "changing" and the letter e is deleted.

Verbs Ending in Y

In most cases, a verb that ends in Y will require you to use a new series of letters depending on the letter that comes right before it. A word with a consonant before the Y will include a change in its form in most cases. "Pry" can become pries, pried or prying. A verb that has a vowel right before the Y at the end will not have many changes. "Pray" will become prays, prayed or praying.

Double Consonants

Double consonants are used to support short vowel sounds within a root word. "Planning" is an example as the noun is utilized to promote the sound of "plan," the root word. A common spelling error is omitting one of the double consonants as in "planing," pronounced with a long "a" and has a different meaning.

Spelling Rules for Vowels

The following rules may be followed:

- The first vowel in a set of two is always the one that dominates the vowel sound in the word. For example, "rain" where the vowel sound is a long "a."

- A vowel may produce a schwa sound within a word that does not have any parts that use stress points.

- "I" before "e" except after "c." *Receive* is a good example.

Silent E

The following rules may be followed when a silent "e" is needed:

- The vowel in the middle of the word has a long sound when the word ends in an "e," as in bone, same, shine.

- Words in the English language do not end in V or U. There are some exceptions to the U rule like gnu and menu, but in almost every other case "e" must be added at the end of the word.

- Each syllable must have a vowel sound.

Additional Spelling Rules

The following additional rules are to be considered when spelling words:

- The c sound will be soft, like an "s" sound, when an e, i or y is used after the s. In other cases, the c is a "k" sound.

- The g sound will be soft, like a "j" sound when it comes before an e, i or y.

- The letter q is always followed by the letter u. This may be seen in words like question, etiquette and quest.

- "Y", when used as a single vowel, will change to an "I" when a suffix is added, as in envy and envies.

Quotations

Quotation marks are needed to indicate a direct quote or to emphasize the words are taken from another source.

The comma should always go within the quotation. A period, question mark or exclamation point may also be included within the quotation mark if applicable. A colon or semicolon should always go outside of the quotation marks.

Using References

References may be used to refer to an item that is not included in the sentence. For instance, "The doctor visited the young boy. He told the boy to drink milk every day." The "he" used in the sentence is the reference as it refers to the doctor.

The reference should not be implied. For example, a sentence may say "The doctor told the boy to drink his milk." The "his" is confusing as it is unclear whether the boy should drink his milk or whether the doctor has a glass of milk too and wants the boy to have that. Also, the word "this" or "that" should not be used if not followed by a noun; the problem is the reader will not understand what the "this" or "that" refers to.

An antecedent is an event or object that occurs prior. The antecedent may be repeated to confirm the information in the reference. In the example listed above, the doctor's identity may be repeated: "The doctor told the boy to drink more milk. The doctor wanted the boy to have a glass every day." The identities of the doctor and the boy are repeated to clarify for the reader what is being discussed.

The content may also be reorganized to allow the referent to be closer to the antecedent. In this case, you may use the sentence "The doctor wants the boy to drink milk." The boy is closer to the doctor in this case as there is a better link between the two figures. Therefore, the reader knows that the doctor is specifically asking the boy to drink milk.

The sentence may also be structured so as to eliminate the need for a referent. In this case: "It was important for the boy to listen to the doctor. He was told by the doctor to drink more milk." The "he" in this case is the boy, as the sentence is organized to let the reader know that it is the doctor telling the boy to drink the milk.

Applying Writing Skills in the Classroom

<u>Planning the Project</u>

A plan is important in writing as it ensures the student understands what the subject matter is. To start, the student may be given instructions on how to complete a task. After that, the student can be given detailed information about the assigned topic. The student should be given time to plan the project.

Defining the Topic

You must help the student define the topic at the beginning of the writing process. For instance, a student may be told to write a paper on a historical event. The topic needs to be specific and name that particular event so that the student keeps to the topic.

Defining the Purpose

"Purpose" refers to the intention a writer has for authoring a paper. A purpose will guide the writer in deciding what the paper will be about and how that content is structured. The purpose may include one of the following:

1. Summary

The student can choose to summarize the document in question by writing about the topic in a few sentences. This includes focusing on the most basic points or most important aspects. Specific details may be ignored. The summary should be written in the writer's own words. That is, the content is not to be directly repeated. Some quotations may be used in the summary, although those are only to be used in cases where the content is a necessity for discussion. A brief news story that has only one or two paragraphs to explain what happened in a certain situation may be a summary of a much larger story, for instance.

2. Description

A description may be used in a writing passage to explain the topic. The description can be about a person, place, event, process or anything else the passage or paper will discuss. A descriptive paper generally provides an opinion.

3. Persuasion

A persuasive document involves encouraging the reader to agree with the writer. The reader should be provided with enough information about the subject matter. Research may also be utilized to bolster the argument. Some examples of persuasive material include newspaper editorials.

4. Compare and Contrast

A compare and contrast paper will look at two or more items and see what makes them alike or different from one another. An example can involve looking at two vehicles of the same class and style that were produced by two different car companies.

5. Instructional

This guides a reader through a series of steps or instructions. A how-to project on how to complete a home improvement task is an example of an instructional report. A guide on how to prepare for a special event is also an example.

Writing Modes

In addition to different purposes, the writer may be expected to work with various modes of writing. These include:

1. Narrative

Narrative is a writing mode that focuses on telling a story. The narrative includes characters and dialogue. An appropriate beginning and ending should be included in the story. Some conflicts, disputes and other problems may also be incorporated into the narrative. The information may provide the reader with an interesting way to learn something. The content has to be gripping and inviting to the reader.

2. Letter

Letters are often used to persuade someone about a certain topic. This may also be used to describe things that happened in the past, present or future. Letters can deal with personal or business topics.

3. Analysis

Analytical writing involves specific information such as statistics. An analysis can be used when talking about scientific points or business-related concepts. Concrete data should be included in the text. The analysis may also include some persuasive elements, but that is optional.

Determining the Audience

The audience that the writer intends to address should be decided before starting to write. The audience may be a very specific group of people or age group, for example. Choosing an audience also involves determining whether writing should be formal or informal. A formal audience may be a group of teachers or bankers, for example. An informal audience could be someone's friends.

The size of the audience and the audience's prior knowledge of the subject matter should also be considered.

Prewriting

Prewriting is a process that involves helping a student develop an argument or understand a topic. The writer will get an idea of what is expected in the writing process. This may include a better understanding of the background involved in a certain situation. The following are types of prewriting:

1. Freewriting

Freewriting is a process where the student writes about anything based on a specific topic. The freewriting practice is designed to let the student not only come up with new ideas but also to see how existing ideas can be expanded. The student should write without worrying about corrections or mistakes. Any content that may be used in the final project can always be revised and edited.

2. Brainstorming

Brainstorming is similar to freewriting, but the main difference is that brainstorming doesn't require complete sentences. Students can write down various keywords that are associated with the topic. The list of words can then be analyzed to see if any specific connections can be made between items. The list of brainstormed items can then be organized as appropriate.

3. Clustering

Clustering involves organizing ideas. A student writes down a keyword that pertains to the assigned topic and then writes relates words all around it, circling words or groups of words and connecting them as appropriate with lines. Then the students write another keyword and repeat the process. The goal of clustering is not only to produce ideas but to visualize how they may be linked together.

4. Outlining

An outline may be used to organize the content for the final writing project. The outline may be used as a table of contents of sorts. In the outline, the writer will create a series of primary points that relate directly to the topic. Those primary points are then broken down into a series of secondary concepts that could provide the framework for each paragraph, for example, designating main ideas, supporting details, etc.

Using Reference Materials

The writer should be encouraged to use various reference materials to support arguments or to find new ideas to include. Students can work with textbooks, journals, websites or any other reliable source that offers information.

1. Reference materials

A website is a good place to start. Such a reference source will give the writer an introduction to the topic. Libraries are also a good resource, as are newspapers, magazines, online scholarly databases, academic journals, etc.

2. Accurate and up-to-date content

Writers should use recent research to develop their writing. This includes using the newest editions of books, newspapers or other periodicals, or websites that are consistently updated. Older resources may be more appropriate for writing that requires historical context, for instance.

3. Authentic sources

The problem with some sources is that they might be questionable in nature. Although websites like Wikipedia have become popular, the fact that such places are edited by the general public makes them hard to trust. Sometimes the information such websites provide is inaccurate. Students should be encouraged to avoid such sites and to focus on more academic, formal resources. Academic journals are among the most trustworthy resources that students may use. However, those resources may also be difficult for some students to understand if they are not overly familiar with the subject matter.

Any type of resource, whether physical or digital, is fine to use so long as it's relevant, reliable and up-to-date (as appropriate to the topic).

Writing a Thesis Statement

The thesis statement is an author's main argument. The thesis statement must be specific and relevant to the subject. It must also be brief—no more than one or two sentences in length.

A thesis statement must be very specific and state the goals of the writer. A vague thesis would be, "I will review two sources that are about cow farming and see how I can combine them into one argument." A more specific and effective thesis would be, "I will analyze the works of (author X) and (author Y) regarding their theories of cow farming. This paper will examine how the authors' theories differ and how they may be combined to provide a more comprehensive, collaborative approach to cow farming." This thesis is a little longer, but it is more specific as it focuses on specific sources and emphasizes the goal of the paper.

The argument must also be unique and presented in such a manner that a reader is clear on what will be discussed. For example, "The developments of (authors X and Y) regarding the cow farming industry will be reviewed. Their opinions will be analyzed as to how they influence the industry and encourage new technologies."

Is a Debate Possible?

While the thesis statement concentrates on introducing the content, it may also elicit a debate about whether a certain theory is better than another, for example.

Watch the Language

A student's thesis should be simple and relatively non-technical. Instead of, "The bovine farming industry must utilize technical advancements in solar technology to allow the industry to thrive and evolve," a better thesis would be, "The cow farming industry may benefit from the use of solar energy to allow for the field's continued growth."

Proper Paragraphs

The writer can use as many paragraphs as needed in the project. However, each paragraph should be dedicated to one aspect of the topic if possible. To organize a paragraph:

1. A topic sentence is needed.

Each paragraph needs a topic sentence that introduces the idea of the paragraph. The topic sentence should be at the beginning of the paragraph. The sentence prepares the reader for whatever will be highlighted in the paragraph.

2. A series of supporting details will bolster the topic sentence.

The supporting details appear after the topic sentence. For instance, the topic sentence might state that a humidifier can keep a home comfortable during the winter season. The supporting details in the paragraph will then focus on why the humidifier is so useful and include appropriate supporting information.

3. The paragraphs should be long enough.

A paragraph needs enough sentences to provide the reader with sufficient information about the topic sentence.

When to Divide Paragraphs

In some cases, the writer might need to write two or more paragraphs based on the same main point. Two arguments in one paragraph should be separated, with each paragraph being as detailed as possible.

Planning Transitions

Transitions are used in documents to move smoothly from one point to the next. Transitions are typically used in documents to indicate that a new idea is being introduced and has some connection to the original main idea of the last paragraph. A transition can include a signal word at the start of a new paragraph or the end of the previous paragraph to state that a new paragraph is going to begin.

Examples of transitions:

1. **Addition**: also, and, again, furthermore, besides and in addition. An example could be, "The chef was proficient in making pastries. In addition to that, the chef could also mix drinks." The transition moves from one of the chef's skills to another.

2. **Similarity**: likewise, also, identically, in the same way. In this case, the writer may state, "The bus was late. Also, the people on the bus were in a hurry." The transition links two conditions present in the same scenario.

3. **Exception:** on the other hand, but, however, in contrast. "Everyone was very happy, but one person still felt that the party could have been better." The word "but" introduces an exception transition.

4. **Sequence:** first, second, third, before, after, while. These transitions indicate order or time.

5. **Giving an Example:** for example, for instance, specifically. These transitions indicate the writer is providing support for whatever main point is being made in a particular paragraph.

6. **Conclusion:** finally, in conclusion, in summary can be used as transitions. For example, "In conclusion, we have found which cheese the participants in the study like the best." In this case, "in conclusion" indicates a summation of the writing or the results of a study.

All transitions should be used cautiously and judiciously. While transitions help guide readers, too many of them can get confusing.

<u>Using a Scholarly Approach to Writing</u>

A scholarly process entails a focus on formal language. This includes ensuring that slang and contractions are avoided and that appropriate vocabulary is used for the topic.

Sentences should not be extremely long. Compound sentences or run-on sentences that try to add too many details at a time should be avoided.

Passive voice should be avoided.

<u>Active and Passive Voice</u>

Active Voice

Active voice is a form of writing that identifies the subject that is participating in a certain action. An example of a sentence using the active voice is, "I wrote an essay." In this sentence, someone or something (the noun or the subject) performs an action (the verb or predicate).

Passive Voice

The passive voice is used to indicate something was done to the subject. For example, "The book was written by James." Active voice would be: "James wrote the book."

The passive voice occurs if "to be" is used in the past tense (was, were). An example of this is "Papers were graded." Active voice is "The teacher graded the papers."

Passive voice is also present when the verb appears before the actor within the sentence. An example here is, "The papers were graded by the teachers." The actor that was responsible for grading the papers is listed at the end of the sentence.

This does not mean that the passive voice should be avoided at all times. There are some cases where people will intentionally use the passive voice. The subject may be included later in the sentence for purposes of de-emphasizing it. An example would be, "The schools that achieve certain test grades will get special rewards according to rules established by the state's governing board." The governing board is the main subject of the sentence, but the focus in this sentence is not on the board. Instead, the focus is on what will happen to the school that achieves specific test grades. Therefore, the board is only listed at the end.

Students are encouraged to be aware of what they're doing when using passive voice. They should name the subject of their sentences before the verb. The students should also be told that the active voice helps make their writing clearer.

<u>Using the Word 'It'</u>

Students often use "it" when writing to shorten a sentence. However, using "it" too many times may cause the main subject of a sentence to be lost. When the uncertain pronoun is used too often, the reader will struggle to figure out what the "it" refers to. The "it" can be any noun that was involved in a prior sentence.

Starting an Introduction

The introduction is the part of the paper that exposes the reader to the content for the first time. An introduction can be a few paragraphs long and explains what the subject matter is. The goal is both to introduce the topic and engage the reader.

The introduction may include a discussion of anything written about the topic in the past or a review of any problems or other points that the writer wishes to address. The introduction may also provide a reason for the writing.

The introduction can be a thesis statement that is designed to be the answer to a problem or the main concept that will be highlighted throughout the writing.

General Introduction Length

The length of the introduction is generally a few paragraphs. The key is to keep the introduction both succinct and informative as well as engaging.

Creating a Conclusion

The conclusion is placed at the very end of the paper. It provides a sense of closure as the reader is reminded of the main points introduced in the paper. In most cases, the conclusion will only need to be one or two paragraphs. The most important main ideas that the writer spent the most time talking about should be briefly revisited. The thesis statement should be introduced once again at the end and the results or findings stated.

The conclusion does not introduce any new content. It's designed to review content, not bring up new ideas. The reader must feel a sense of closure. In other words, the reader should not be left hanging.

Drafting, Editing and Revising

The drafting process is the process of revising one's writing. The writer is expected to produce multiple drafts of the same work. The goal is for each draft to be better than the next.

The first draft is the preliminary paper. This is not the version that is to be graded. A teacher should provide feedback to a student which allows the writer to understand what should be done to enhance the content or correct errors.

Considerations for Revision

Each paragraph should only include one clear main idea. Proper transitions should be noted in between paragraphs even if the paragraphs are about the same topic or concept.

The voice used in the writing process should also be consistent throughout. Any specific rules involving the assignment should be followed. All sources should also be cited.

The writer should plan enough time to revise the paper.

Revising for Focus

One of the most common revisions is the writing's focus. The student's focus may not be clear. The main topic should be what is discussed, rather than extraneous details.

Revising to Strengthen a Statement

Some narrative or argumentative statements may be weak in the first draft of a paper. Relevant sources may be added to correct a weak statement. The writer can add one or more arguments depending on what that person feels is appropriate for discussion. The argument should be relevant to the subject.

Revising Grammatical Errors

Grammatical errors include gender agreement, verb tenses, subject and verb agreement, word usage and spelling.

As the student goes through the revision process, the student will begin to notice trends in terms of errors. For example, a student may find he or she struggles with switching between tenses. Identifying such issues allows them to be corrected in future drafts.

Students can use a website such as Grammarly to get information on how well their writing follows grammatical rules. A website like this will review any possible errors in the writing. Such websites may help identify problems in a student's work. It's important to note, however, that Grammarly is also known to make mistakes.

Making an Argument

An argument is the opinion that the writer is stating or the point the writer is making. This could be an opinion relating to a debate or a personal belief. Sometimes the argument will aim to convince the reader that a certain view is correct or wrong. The most persuasive arguments are always backed up by facts and evidence.

The most important part of making an argument is to keep the content from being negative. The content should not be emotional or overtly opinionated. The focus should be factual and measured in terms of word choice.

Common Types of Arguments

An argument is typically listed as either deductive or inductive. A deductive argument involves weighing evidence to determine what makes a conclusion true. An inductive argument starts with a conclusion, such as a prediction, and the argument is then worked around that premise.

Three Elements of an Argument

Each argument that a writer produces will contain three specific elements:

1. Claim: This is the main point that the writer wants to discuss. The claim is often a thesis statement.

2. Support: This is the evidence supporting the claim. It can involve research as discussed earlier, such as academic journals, websites, etc.

3. Warrant: This is a definition involving the claim.

Fallacies

The writer must be cautious when making an argument in order to avoid fallacies. A fallacy is an issue that causes an argument to become invalid. For instance, a writer might make a generalization assuming that all things in a certain subject have the same qualities and characteristics as one another. Another fallacy may involve a lack of a logical relationship between two concepts.

Bias and Objectivity

Objectivity is a practice where a person writes as fairly and neutrally as possible. Objective writing helps establish trust with a reader and avoids alienating an audience. Objective writing involves avoiding bias as much as possible.

Bias is a person's attitudes or preferences. A person might write with certain assumptions. Some of the more common forms of bias include:

- Cases where the writer uses an all-or-nothing description; this includes assuming that all people within a certain group agree or disagree

- Instances where there is no evidence

- Instances where the writer makes an assumption involving specific subjects based on past (potentially outdated) evidence

- A person being too sympathetic or supportive of a specific figure or viewpoint in a story.

For instance, "The teacher should recognize her role in helping students" would be wrong as this creates the bias or assumption suggesting that all teachers are women. In the sentence, "Teachers should understand their role in helping students" is better as this does not create ambiguity and is gender-neutral. That is, the writer indicates that teachers can be male or female.

A sentence like "The senior population in the city is rapidly growing" could come across as biased given that there's no evidence offered. A better sentence could include research such as, "The senior population in the city has grown by approximately 25 percent in the past three years (source citation)."

Completing the Writing Portion of the Test

The ParaPro test includes several types of questions. You may be required to analyze certain words or to assess how sentences are constructed. You may also be told to analyze certain passages and answer questions or find errors.

Spelling Questions

You will come across some questions during the ParaPro test that focus on spelling. These include questions where you will have to identify which of four words is spelled incorrectly. Refer to the spelling rules listed earlier in the chapter.

Be aware of how the plural of a word is formed or how a word might sound as it is written. Look at how the suffix in a word is added based on the desired meaning. Make sure you look at how double consonants are arranged. You also have to look at how the word is spelled based on its definition and placement in the sentence.

Parts of Speech Questions

A question regarding the parts of speech requires you to answer a question relating to word usage. You may be asked to indicate which word is a noun, adjective, verb, adverb, etc.

Be aware of whether the word in question is a name, place or idea, as that word would be a noun. Meanwhile, a word that lists an action is a verb. An adjective will describe a noun, and an adverb will explain a verb.

Sentence Analysis Questions

A sentence analysis question will feature a sentence that includes four underlined parts. You must review each underlined part and decide which is the subject and which is the predicate. You may also be required to identify separate words, such as the noun(s), verb, adjective(s), adverb(s) or the object of the sentence. You may notice a certain part of the sentence is incorrect. The underlined parts of a sentence may include not only parenthetical parts but also multiple words at a time. Be sure that each part of the sentence connects with the next and that everything is in the same tense or voice.

Review the errors you find and decide what you can do to correct the issue. You may need to use a different word or a different tense. In other cases, you may have to change the punctuation. Sometimes the correct answer is to remove the error altogether and not add anything new.

Reviewing Parts of a Sentence

You may also be asked to review an entire sentence. You may be presented with the sentence, "The baker worked hard on getting the doughnuts ready." You could be asked which part of the sentence is the subject, complete predicate, verb, adverb, etc. You may also be asked to identify other types of words within the sentence.

The test will not require you to write anything unique or to use your imagination to create a passage.

Writing Questions

1. What word in this sentence is the adverb? "The conservative approach was quickly implemented as a safe approach."

    a. conservative

    b. approach

    c. quickly

    d. implemented

2. What word in this sentence is the adjective? "The football team was near the end zone during the massive game."

    a. team

    b. near

    c. football

    d. massive

3. Which word in this sentence is a preposition? "Sam left for the beach before his neighbors could."

    a. left

    b. for

    c. before

    d. his

4. Which word in these sentences is an interjection? "The pitcher threw a perfect game. Amazing!"

    a. pitcher

    b. threw

    c. perfect

    d. amazing

5. Correct the underlined portion of this sentence: "Shannon had come out to the party."

    a. arrived

    b. came

    c. has come out

    d. had come in

6. Correct the underlined part of this sentence: "<u>Whose</u> trying to open the door?

    a. Who's

    b. Whose is

    c. Who's in

    d. Whose in

7. Identify the part that is incorrect in this sentence: "The baseball team were very fast, but the team doesn't know how to hit."

    a. were

    b. (comma use)

    c. doesn't

    d. how to

8. What type of clause is used in this sentence? "Because the weather was rough, the beach had to close down for the day."

    a. Dependent

    b. Adverb

    c. Adjective

    d. Independent

9. The following word can be used as a noun in a gerund phrase:

    a. Hiking

    b. Accommodating

    c. Wasting

    d. Anticipating

10. What is the error in the following sentence? "The fortune teller could feel the spirit's presents."

    a. feel

    b. spirit's

    c. presents

    d. (period usage)

Refer to the following passage for Questions 11-13:

The doctor reviewed his notes on the patient. He was confused over what he could do with that person. He thought about the other patients he had treated and wondered what he could have done to fix the problems. He could not wait, he had to take action.

11. What is the point of view of the narrator in this passage?

    a. First person

    b. Second person

    c. Third person

    d. Third person omnipresent

12. Which word in this passage is an adjective?

    a. Reviewed

    b. Confused

    c. Treated

    d. Wait

13. What error can be found in this passage?

    a. Incorrect spelling

    b. Tense changes or shifts

    c. Run-on sentence

    d. Improper comma use

14. A synonym for speedy would be:

    a. Slow

    b. Questionable

    c. Quick

    d. Active

15. A summary in writing is designed to:

    a. Confirm details on something that the student is reading

    b. Influence a person to make a decision

    c. Describe in detail what something is like

    d. Explain a theory

16. A letter writing style involves the writer:

    a. Directly addressing a certain person or group

    b. Describing things in the past tense

    c. Being personal in one's prose

    d. All of the above

17. Brainstorming and freewriting are both types of prewriting. What makes the two different from each another?

   a. The length of the content

   b. The sentences written

   c. How detailed the content may be

   d. The subject matter

18. At most, how long should an introduction be?

   a. 3 pages

   b. 8 pages

   c. 1 page

   d. Half a page

19. Which of these points is not a part of an argument in a written work?

   a. Claim

   b. Warrant

   c. Support

   d. Suggestion

20. A deductive argument in writing involves making a conclusion true by:

    a. Finding out what evidence will make that conclusion true

    b. Working with reason

    c. Guessing what may happen

    d. Asking people for information on the subject matter

Answers

1. c. Quickly is an adverb, *conservative* is an adjective, *approach* is a noun and *implemented* is a verb in the past tense.
2. d. *Massive* is an adjective. The *football team* and the *end zone* are both nouns. *Near* is an adverb that links the football team and end zone.
3. c. *Before* is used to let the reader know that Sam's action took place prior to when his neighbor's action occurred.
4. d. *Amazing* is added to the end of the statement to say that the pitcher's action was outstanding.
5. b. *Came* is a more precise and concise version of "had come out." This also uses fewer words and is easier to read.
6. a. *Who's* is the only sensible option, although that may be written as "who is" if you wish. The apostrophe is placed in the correct position in this situation.
7. a. "Were" should be replaced with "was." "Were" refers to a plural item, while "was" refers to a singular noun.
8. b. This is an adverb clause as "Because" reminds the reader of why the beach was closed.
9. a. Hiking can be used as a noun in a gerund phrase like "Hiking is a very enjoyable activity." The word is a verb that becomes a noun.
10. c. "Presents" is an example of a word being used improperly. Instead of "presents," the word should be "presence." This is an example of two words that are pronounced similar to one another but have different meanings.

11. d. This is a third person omnipresent narration in that the doctor's feelings can be identified.
12. b. *Confused* is an adjective as it explains the doctor's feelings. *Reviewed* and *treated* are past-tense verbs. *Wait* is used as a noun.
13. d. The last sentence in the passage uses a comma incorrectly. A semicolon should be used in this case.
14. c. A synonym is a word that may substitute for another word without changing the definition or meaning of the sentence.
15. a. The summary briefly explains the main points discussed in the writing.
16. d. A letter is a communication to a certain person and can be written using personal language depending on the subject matter. The letter may also include information on things that happened in the past or what the writer wants to do.
17. b. Both options allow the writer to be specific and to talk about anything relating to the prompt. Freewriting involves writing a document off-hand, and brainstorming involves the writer listing ideas. No full sentences are required when brainstorming.
18. a. Although a shorter introduction is best, an introduction can be three pages in length if an extensive amount of explanation is required about the subject matter.
19. d. A suggestion is not used in an argument. The content must be supported with the evidence needed for making a statement.
20. a. Deduction may be used to review the subject matter. Various resources or reference materials and even test items can be used to determine what is true.

Section 3: Mathematics

The mathematics segment of the ParaPro exam focuses on how well you understand various concepts in the field of mathematics. Part of the test is technical in nature, based on calculations that must be completed when solving certain math problems. You are expected to understand the relationships between different numbers and how calculations are made.

You must also recognize how to apply mathematics to solve equations. You will be required to know the formulas for certain calculations, such as finding the area, volume, perimeter and circumference of certain shapes. You are not allowed to use a calculator during the ParaPro exam.

The first segment focuses on understanding the general principles of math, how numbers can be manipulated and how they relate to each other. You may eventually move on to other subjects like geometry and algebra after you focus on the basic parts of math.

Types of Numbers

Integers

You are expected to identify the various kinds of numbers that students will come across. The basic numbers are integers. 0 may also be seen as an integer. An integer is not a fraction or decimal. A digit would be a single number on its own. All ten basic single numbers from 0 to 9 are digits.

Consecutive integers are integers that follow one another in the same sequence. These integers may be highlighted by the following: n, n+1, n+2, etc. For instance, n may be 28, thus leading to the consecutive integers 28, 29, 30 and so forth.

Integers may be arranged on a number line. The line is a visual layout of all the whole numbers in a row. The line might include 11 points from -5 to 5. Each point would be a whole number, with 0 being in the center. You may use this to illustrate to students how certain numbers relate to one another on the number line.

Integers may also be referred to as whole numbers because there are no decimals or fractions involved. However, whole numbers are positive integers. You can still use a number line to illustrate the whole numbers that students may use. The line will produce a visual representation of which numbers are larger than one another. The line can also use those whole numbers in addition and subtraction equations.

Odd, Even and Prime Numbers

You should be able to identify odd, even and prime numbers. Odd numbers cannot be divided by 2, such as 1, 3, 5 and so forth. Even numbers can be divided by 2, such as 2, 4, 12, 100. An even number can be divided by 2 to create a whole number. 0 is not an even number.

A prime number is one that cannot be divided to produce a full integer; it cannot result in a whole number and a fraction less than 1. The number 1 is not a prime number; 2 is the only even prime number.

Factors are numbers that are divisors of integers. For instance, the numbers 1, 2 and 4 are all factors of 8. You can divide 8 by any of those numbers to produce an integer.

3 would not be a factor of 8 because dividing 8 by 3 would result in a whole number plus a decimal or a fraction.

A multiple is a product that is produced between an integer and another integer. For instance, the multiples of 3 include -6, -3, 0, 3, 6, 9, 12, 15 and so forth. 0 is the only integer that is a multiple of every single number.

Critical Numbers

Decimal Point

A decimal point may be noticed at the end of a number. Everything to the left of the decimal point is a number that is determined to a power of 10. For instance, the number 13.25 would include the 1 and is to the power of 10. The 3 is to the power of 1. The 10 and 3 are combined together to get a 13. For the points to the right of the decimal point, the 2 is to the power of -1 and the 5 is to the power of -10. This means that the number is not negative, but rather a small part of the original integer.

Positioning of Numbers (Place Value)

Numbers can be placed alongside one another in any manner. You can write a number that has as many digits as needed. However, the numbers will have different place values depending on where they are situated. For instance, the number 85 features the digits 8 and 5. Those two digits have different values based on their positions.

In the instance of 85, the 8 is in the tens position. This means that the number's value is 80. The number 5 is in the ones' position and has a value of 5.

The place values of numbers are as follows for the number 15,348,792:

1 = tens of millions

5 = millions

3 = hundred thousands

4 = ten thousands

8 = thousands

7 = hundreds

9 = tens

2 = ones

In this example, the number would be recited as "fifteen million, three hundred and forty-eight thousand, seven hundred and ninety-two." The numbers are in the correct order based on their place values. The largest number is always the one that comes first. In the case of the example, 1 and 5 are the first numbers because they refer to the millions that are involved in the total. The layout can be used for as long as a number persists; you may come across the billions and trillions values as well.

A decimal point is the period that appears in the middle of a whole number. A decimal is formed when there are numbers on both sides of the period. The decimal will have additional place values to go alongside what was introduced earlier in the number.

Any numbers that appear after a decimal point will be designated as tenths, hundredths, thousandths and so forth. In the example 15.792, 1 and 5 are in the tens' and ones' spots. 7 is in the tenths, 9 is in the hundredths and 2 is in the thousandths. A number can have as many positions after the decimal point as needed. In most cases, a student can round the total to the nearest decimal point; 15.7926 can be rounded to 15.793 if you want to round it to the nearest thousandth, 15.79 to the nearest hundredth or 15.8 to the nearest tenth.

Basic Mathematics Functions

<u>Addition</u>

Addition involves adding whole numbers that occupy the same place. For instance, you may have the equation 15 + 42. The digits must be aligned so that the numbers in the ones' place and tens place are under each other respectively. You add 5 and 2 at the start to produce 7 ones. Then you add 1 by 4 to get 5 tens. The 5 is in the 10s place.

You may also carry values in an addition problem. This is for cases where the sum of two numbers in the ones' place equals 10 or more. In this example, we will use the equation 15 + 47. You would add the 5 and 7 ones to equal one 10 and two ones. The ten is transferred or carried over to the tens place and added to the numbers already in the tens place, which are 1 and 4. The total number in the tens place is now 6. So you have 6 tens and 2 ones or 62.

You may also carry values if they are 20 or higher. This is for cases where you are adding three or more numbers together. When you use the equation 25 + 59 + 48, the second numbers in each integer are added together to produce 22, which is 2 tens and 2 ones. You would transfer or carry the 2 tens over to the tens place and 2, 5, 4 and 2 to equal 13. The answer is 13 tens and 2 ones or 132.

Subtraction

Subtraction is the opposite of addition, such as 5 − 3 = 2. You can use the same principles for addition as you would for subtraction when working with larger numbers. You would take 578 − 432 by subtracting each number in their respective position from one another (8-2, 7-3, 5-4). This would give you the final result of 146.

Whereas addition requires carrying numbers over to the next position, subtraction requires borrowing. You have to recognize the places of each digit, whether it is in a one, ten, or hundreds place, and ensure you don't write numbers incorrectly so that the digits are misaligned.

For example, in 845 − 677, recognize that 5 and 7 are in the ones' place, 4 and 7 are in the tens place and 8 and 6 are in the hundreds place. The number 5 is not large enough to take 7 away, so you borrow a ten from the digit to the left. Now you have 15 ones minus 7 equals 8 ones. You have 3 tens left in the tens place (because you borrowed a ten) and 3 tens is not enough to take 7 away. So you have to borrow one hundred from the 8 hundred to the left. Now you can subtract 7 tens from 13 tens to equal 6 tens. Now you have 7 hundreds minus 6 hundreds to equal 1 hundred. The final answer is 1 hundred, 6 tens and 8 ones which is 168.

Multiplication and Multiplication Tables

Multiplication involves adding a number to itself many times over. This is an extended form of addition. For instance, 3 x 5 = 15 is the same as 3 + 3 + 3 + 3 + 3 = 15.

The process of identifying the product in a multiplication process requires multiplying each individual number in every position. The process involves taking partial products and adding them together to produce a final result.

For example, you may come across the equation 15 x 5. You would multiply 5 x 5 in the ones' column to get 25. The 2 is then carried over to the tens column. You would then multiply 1 x 5 to get 5 and then add 2 tens to produce 7. The two columns are combined to create the final product of 75.

It gets more complicated when dealing with numbers with multiple digits, such as the equation 25 x 16. You would take the 6 on the second part and multiply that by each number in 25. 6 x 5 = 30 and results in the ones' column having a 0 and the 3 being added to the end of 6 x 2. You would get a final result of 150. For the next part, you would add a 0 to the end to emphasize that the 25 x 1 part starts in the tens. In this case, you would have a total of 250. By adding 150 with 250, you get a final product of 400.

Anything that is multiplied by 0 will give you an answer of 0. In the equation 452 x 105, you would multiply 452 by 5 to get 2260, but you would skip the tens' spot because 452 x 0 is 0. But you would continue to the hundreds spot to multiply 452 by 1 while adding the two zeros to get 45,200, thus producing the final product of 47,460.

Multiplication Tables

A multiplication table can be depicted on a horizontal and vertical axis. It will have numbers from 1 to 12 or greater on one axis and the same numbers on the other axis. All the intersections between the two axes will produce a number. For instance, a student will go to the 7 spot on one axis and then move to the 9 spot on the other axis to find 63. The student can review the table based on how certain multiples of a number change. The 4 column will show the numbers 4, 8, 12, 16, 20 and so forth to illustrate the multiples of that number. Multiplication tables should be memorized, as in the 4 times table, the 8 times table, etc.

Division

Division is an extended form of subtraction. You are taking a number and then dividing it by another total or the divisor. How many times can that divisor be subtracted from the original number? In this case, 12/3 is asking how many 3s there are in 12 and the answer is 4. That is, you would subtract 3 from 12 four times before reaching 0.

In some cases, you may come across a remainder. This is for cases where you can't divide a number by another to produce a full integer. For instance, you may come across the equation 140/13. In other words, how many 13s are in 140? The answer would be 10 with a remainder of 10. This means that you can subtract 13 from 140 a total of 10 times, but you will be left with a remainder of 10.

Odd and Even Numbers in Addition and Multiplication

The result of an addition or multiplication problem will be an odd or even number. When two even numbers are added or multiplied, the result is even. When two odd numbers are added, the sum is also even. But when two odd numbers are multiplied, the product is also odd. When an even and odd number are added to each other, the sum is odd. When an even and odd number are multiplied, the product is even.

Signed Numbers in Multiplication and Division

When a positive number is multiplied by a negative number, the product is a negative number. When two negative numbers are multiplied, the product is a positive number. For instance, -5 x -4 would equal +20. For division, a positive number divided by a negative number will create a negative answer. The same total can be found when a negative number is divided by a positive one.

As with multiplication, two negative numbers in a division equation will result in a positive answer. If -20 were divided by -5, the answer would be +4.

Advanced Math Functions

Decimals

A decimal is a number that includes digits in the tenth, hundredth or thousandth positions, etc. The decimal number is not a whole number, but rather a portion of a whole number. For instance, the number 14.65 contains a whole number and a decimal number. The 6 is in the tenths position and the 5 is in the hundredths spot. The rules for the digits to the left of the decimal point are 1 in the tens position and 4 in the ones' position.

The general process of calculating basic equations with decimals is the same as with whole numbers. But you must be aware of the decimal spot for each question. For instance, 14.65 + 18.156 would require the student to expand how the numbers are laid out. The problem can be solved as 14.650 + 18.156. That is, the first number will have a 0 in the thousandths spot. Although it has no value, the 0 is needed to simplify the process of calculating the equation, thus producing a correct answer of 32.806.

For multiplication, decimals are aligned based on their final digits. For instance, a student might multiple 4.5 by 3.69. The digits are aligned with one another on the paper. The decimal point is then moved to include a thousandths place. When two decimals are multiplied, the student adds the number of decimal places in each number to determine the number of decimal places in the product of the multiplication. In the example of 4.5 x 3.69, there are three decimal places so the answer will have three places. The answer or product will be calculated to the thousandth, thus producing the answer 16.605.

For division, the divisor is moved to the right to create a whole number and the decimal of the number to be divided will also be moved the exact number of digits to the right. For example, with 2.35 ÷1.5, the divisor (1.5) will become 15 and the number to be divided will become 23.5 or 23.500 to produce the answer of 1.566.

Exponents

An exponent is a number indicating that a number is multiplied by itself. If a number is squared or cubed, the number is multiplied by itself two or three times. For instance, 3^2 is 3 x 3, which equals 9, 4^2 = 16, 6^2 = 36, or 8^6 is 8 multiplied by itself 6 times, which equals 262,144. The 6 in this number is called the exponent and is always written smaller and as a superscript.

Radicands and Square Roots

The square root of a number refers to a number that will produce the square root when that number is multiplied by itself. For instance, the square root of 36 is 6 (6x6=36). The 6 is called the index in this equation and 36 is the radicand.

Cubes

In addition to squared exponents and square roots, you may also come across cubed numbers or cube roots. A cubed number is a number that is multiplied by itself three times. The number is represented with an exponent of 3. For example, 3 cubed is $3^3 = 27$ or 3 x 3 x 3.

A cube root occurs when you are determining a number that is multiplied three times to get a certain number. The cube root of 27 is 3, for instance. The cube root is not used as often as a square root.

Fractions

A decimal may be expressed as a fraction. A fraction uses a numerator that is divided by a denominator. For instance, 0.6667 is a decimal number and can be expressed as a fraction by dividing it by 10000 (the same number of zeros as the numerator has places).

A mixed number may also be produced with a whole number and a fraction. For example, 5/3 (an improper fraction; the numerator has a higher value than the denominator) will be written as 1 2/3 (5÷3). When the numerator has a higher value than the denominator, the value is an improper fraction.

Equivalent Fractions

Equivalent fractions are two fractions that are equal to each other but have different numerators and denominators. For instance, 5/12 is the same as 10/24. These are equivalent in that they both divide to the same result of 0.41667. The 10/24 fraction may be reduced to 5/12.

This is to create two or more fractions that can be added, subtracted, multiplied or divided. These calculations cannot be done unless the fractions have the same denominators.

Multiplying Fractions

Two fractions can be cross-multiplied. This is when the numerator of one fraction is multiplied by the denominator of the other. The process is then repeated for the other two numbers that are left. For example, when multiplying 7/11 by 6/13, the first step is to multiply 7 by 13 to equal 91. 91 is the numerator of the equation. Then 11 is multiplied by 6 to equal 66. 66 is the denominator of the equation. The fraction produced is 91/66. This is an improper fraction and must be reduced to its simplest form by dividing 91 by 66 which equals 1 35/66.

Adding and Subtracting Fractions

Adding and subtracting fractions requires fractions to have the same denominator. For instance, in the equation 5/8 + 2/3, the common denominator is a common multiple of 8 and 3, which is 24. The new equation is 15/24 + 16/24. The sum of this is 31/24, which is an improper fraction and is reduced to 1 7/24. The fraction should be reduced to the smallest possible value; 7/24 cannot be reduced any further as the numerator is odd.

The same principle will work for the subtraction process. For 2/3 − 5/8, the fractions are once again expanded to produce 16/24 − 15/24, thus generating the final answer of 1/24. But for 3/5 − 2/6 to have the same denominators, the fractions would be 15/30 − 10/30, which equals 5/30, which is reduced to its simplest form of 1/6.

For multiplication, any mixed numbers should be expressed as improper fractions. The numerators are multiplied separately from the denominators. For 1 2/3 x 4/5, the equation will become 5/3 x 4/5. The numerators are multiplied to equal 20 and the denominators are multiplied to equal 15. The product will be 20/15, which can be converted to 1 5/15, which is then simplified to 1 1/3.

The process of dividing fractions involves mixed numbers first being converted into improper fractions if there are any. The divisor should then be inverted and the final result being multiplied. For example, 3 1/5 ÷ 1/5 and 3 1/5 will become 16/5 and 1/5 is inverted to read 5/1. The totals are then multiplied with one another to create 80/5, which can be reduced to 16.

Percentages

The percentage of a number refers to the hundredths out of 100. For instance, 60% means that you would divide 60 by 100 to get 0.6. There may be times when the percentage of something is greater than 100%. In this case, there will be a whole number combined with a decimal. 150% would be produced by taking 150 and dividing it by 100.

To calculate the percentage, multiply the number in question by the decimal representation of the percentage. The student may be asked to find 30% of 500. The number

500 is multiplied by 0.30. This will produce the final answer of 150. That is, 150 is 30% of 500.

In some cases, you might be asked to calculate the whole of a number when given the percentage. For instance, you may be asked to calculate 85% of 500 which is 85/100 or .85 x 500 = 425. Another example is "If 425 is 85% of a number, what is the number?" This is calculated as 425 ÷ .85 x 100.

Estimation

The estimation process is used to get toward a certain number within a specific digit. As an example, imagine that a person has to estimate a number to the nearest thousandth. For example, a person may need to round 15,345 to the nearest thousandth. The first 5 is in the thousands place. Since 15,345 is closer to 15,000 than 16,000, the correct answer for the estimation is 15,000.

Some questions may require the student to convert a number to the nearest digit. For instance, the student could come across the question 0.657 x 56 while rounding to the nearest hundredth. The correct answer is 36.792. By rounding to the nearest hundredth, the student will obtain the answer 36.79. The process is particularly useful for cases where there are multiple decimal points.

In some cases, the student will have to round up or down. If the student rounds 16.5356 up to the nearest hundredth, the answer will be 16.54. If the student rounds the number down, the answer will be 16.53. The number may also be rounded up to the highest hundredth, which would produce the answer 16.54.

Fractions are not included in the estimation process.

Mean, Median and Mode

The mean is the average (the sum of a series of numbers divided by the total number of numbers). For example, to find the average of 2, 5, 8, 15 and 18, the numbers would be added and divided by 5 and the answer would be 9.6.

The median is the value of the middle number. In 2, 6, 18, 12, 17, 15 and 20, the student must reorganize those numbers in numerical order, which is 2, 6, 12, 15, 17, 18 and 20. The median is 15, the middle number. The median should be found in cases where there is an odd amount of numbers in the line.

For cases where there is an even total of numbers, the median is calculated by adding the two middle numbers and then dividing them by 2. For example, in the series 5, 7, 14, 18, 22 and 30, the two middle numbers are 14 and 18. The two are added together to equal 32 and then divided by 2 to equal 16. Therefore, the median in this situation would be 16.

In some cases, you may be required to round the mean or median to the nearest whole number. The rounding process is more likely to be useful if you have a larger amount of numbers to work with or an even total of numbers and are trying to calculate the median.

The mode is the most-repeated number in a group. A sequence may list 15, 18, 20, 20, 22, 25, 25, 25, 31 and 32. Notice that 25 appears three times and 20 is listed twice. Since 25 is the most frequently occurring number in the sequence, the mode is 25.

The mean, median and mode are often used in cases where statistical information is to be analyzed. This includes cases where several variables or points are measured against one another. The mean and median can create a benchmark for what can be seen, while the mode gives the reader an idea of what might be noticed in the middle part of the equation.

Weighted Average

The weighted average in a sequence requires all data points to be added together. Some numbers are worth more than others. An example of this is: "If you drive for 40 miles per hour for 60 minutes and then drive for 50 miles per hour for 90 minutes, what was your average speed during the 150 minutes?" The average is not 45 miles per hour because the two totals are not equal to one another.

The weighted average shows that 50 miles per hour is more valuable as it took more time. Therefore, the question may be listed as (40(60) + 50(90)) / 150. The two numbers in the numerator become 2400 + 4500, which results in 6,900. That total is divided by 150. The correct answer is 46, as in the driver went 46 miles per hour on average. The person spent more time driving at 50 miles per hour than the person did when going 40 miles per hour.

Order of Operations

The order of operations refers to the order in which calculations must be performed in an equation in order to obtain the correct answer. We will use the problem $18 - 8 + (5 \times 4^2 - 15)$ as an example.

1. The equation in the parentheses must be resolved first. In this equation, the ($5 \times 4^2 - 15$) is calculated first.

2. The exponents are solved next. The 4^2 is 16. Therefore, the end of the equation is now ($5 \times 16 - 15$).

3. Multiplication and division should be calculated next. 5×16 should be calculated to equal 80. All multiplication and division should go from left to right. Remember that anything in the parentheses is still solved first.

4. After this, all addition or subtraction is done from left to right, with anything remaining in parentheses being solved first. The $80 - 15$ becomes 65, thus resulting in $18 - 8 + 65$. The total will be 75.

The acronym PEMDAS is used to help students remember this:

1. Parentheses
2. Exponents
3. Multiplication
4. Division
5. Addition
6. Subtraction

Advanced Sequences

As discussed earlier, a sequence is whole numbers or integers that are in consecutive order (34, 35, 36, 37 …). An advanced sequence will be separated by more than just 1. For instance, an advanced sequence will include additions of 6. This would result in the total of (n + 6), (n + 6 + 6), (n + 6 + 6 + 6) and so forth. The sequence would be listed as 24, 30, 36, 42, 48, 54 … The "…" at the end means that the sequence will go on forever.

The advanced sequence can be any grouping of numbers as long as each number is separated by a common term. In order to answer problems, students must identify what a particular sequence is. One sequence may be listed as 7, 15, 23, 31, 39 … This means that the number beforehand is added by 8 to create the next number. Therefore, the sequence can continue as 47, 55, 63, 71 …

A geometric sequence occurs when the numbers in the sequence have the same multiplier or divisor. An example would be 1, 3, 9, 27 … The sequence shows that the numbers are multiplied by three. The sequence will continue as 81, 243, 729 …

Some other advanced sequences require very specific changes. An example is 8, 20, 34, 50 … The student may notice that 12 was added to 8, and then 14 was added to 20, and 16 was added to 34. The sequence entails adding two more than what was used in each number. The sequence will continue with 18 being added to 50 to get 68 and then 20 added to 68 to produce 88. The sequence can keep on going as 110, 134, 160, 188 …

Identifying Mathematical Symbols

All mathematical symbols are used to represent certain actions that are conducted when resolving certain math problems. For instance, = means that an equation is equal to a certain number. ≠ means that the equation is not equal to the number. The two symbols may be used for all types of processes, including addition and subtraction among others.

When reviewing the differences between results, < means that something is less than another total and > means that a number or equation is greater. You may also find a small line under the < and > symbols. ≤ means that the number before the symbol is less than or equal to the other number on the right.

Basic Math Terms

Basic math terms are traditionally found in word problems. Your students need to know this terminology in order to solve equations. The following are common terms that all students must be able to identify:

- **Sum** – The sum is the product of two numbers that are added together.

- **Difference** – The difference is the result of a subtraction equation.

- **Product** – When two numbers are multiplied by one another, the answer is the product.

- **Quotient** – When you divide one number by another, the answer is the quotient.

- **Numerator** – The numerator is the number that is above the line in a fraction.

- **Denominator** – The denominator is the number below the line in a fraction.

Solving Word Problems

A word problem introduces a situation that requires an equation to be solved. An example of this would be "George has 20 apple crates in his truck. Each apple crate can hold 20 apples. George has room for 8 more apple crates. What is the maximum number of apples that George can carry in his truck?" By reviewing the details, the student will see that George can get 28 apple crates into his truck, each filled with 20 apples. By multiplying 20 by 28, the student will learn that George's truck can carry up to 560 apples at a time.

The student must review the word problem to find the information that is needed. In the example above, the student has to figure out how many apples George can carry with him in his truck. The student will then look at the operations that are needed. The analysis of the question shows that addition is needed to determine the number of crates involved: 20 crates and the 8 additional crates. Multiplication is then needed to multiply the 28 crates by the 20 apples that each crate can hold (28 x 20 = 560), thus producing the final answer of 560 apples.

In other cases, a word problem may be simplified with brief information. The problem may state, "What is the difference between 53 and 35?" The information shows that the student needs to subtract the two numbers. The student will then use the equation 53 – 35 to produce 18. The word "difference" is the key part of the word problem as it focuses on the specific action that must be taken to answer the problem.

Algebra

Algebra is an advanced form of mathematics that is taught in high school or advanced classes in middle school or junior high. Algebra involves manipulating variables and the relationships of numbers with one another. Part of algebra involves missing variables.

Linear Equations

Linear equations are a basic aspect of algebra used to help calculate an unknown number, a variable listed as a letter, commonly x or y.

For instance, a student may find the equation $5 + x = 16$. To solve the equation, the student will subtract 5 from 16 to get 11. This fills in the variable to produce $5 + 11 = 16$. Another way to do this is to subtract the same value from both sides of the equation. By subtracting 5 from $5 + x$, the student will get x. 5 is also subtracted from 16, thus creating $x = 11$. This process is for addition; the opposite is done for subtraction by adding a total to each side (for $x - 15 = 6$, 15 is added to each side to get $x = 21$).

For multiplication, a problem may be listed as $5x = 45$. The variable is isolated by dividing each side by the number that is attached to the variable. In this case, 45 is divided by 5 to get 9. Therefore, $x = 9$.

The variable can only be worth one very specific number within the equation. The variable may be of multiple values if a $\leq$ or $\geq$ symbol is incorporated into the equation. A word problem may also include words like "at least" or "fewer than" or other code words that suggest that the variable can change values in various totals.

Division involves both sides of the equation being multiplied by the same value. For x/3 = 5, the two sides are multiplied by 3. The 5 will become 15 while the denominator on the other side is eliminated, thus creating the answer x = 15. For cases when the variable is the divisor, the other side is divided by the numerator. 15/x = 3 is an example of this. 15 is divided by 3 to get 5, which becomes the variable to create 15/5 = 3, or x = 5.

Linear equations may also be used when solving word problems. Students should review the word problem for key information. For instance, a word problem will state, "What number has to be multiplied by 16 to get 184?" The student will use that information to produce the equation 16x = 184. By dividing 184 by 16, the student will get the correct answer of 11.5.

Inequalities

Inequalities in algebra concentrate on identifying things that are larger or smaller than one another. The < and > signs identify numbers that are larger or smaller than one another. In many cases, the process of solving inequalities will not necessarily produce a definite answer. However, a definite answer is required in cases where an equation has the possibility of being equal to something. This occurs when the ≤ and ≥ symbols are involved.

You may have an algebraic equation that says x + 9 > 16. The x variable has to be something that allows the part on the left to be larger than 16. By subtracting 9 from 16, you will find that x can be 7. But for this equation, the answer has to be x > 7. Therefore, any number that is above 7, including a smaller decimal number like 7.00001, will qualify for the variable.

You may come across the ≤ and ≥ symbols in some of these equations. In one case, an equation may state 5x ≤ 22. You would take 22 and divide that by 5 to get 4.4. This leads to the correct answer of x ≤ 4.4. This means that the variable could be 4.4 and the equation would still be accurate. However, any number that is larger than 4.4 would produce the wrong answer.

In other cases, the variable may be found on the right side of the equation. An example would be 15 < x + 12. You can work with the same process for solving the inequality regardless of the side the variable is on. Subtract 12 from each side, in this case, to find that x = 3. You have the option to flip the sign around to produce x > 3 to continue to state that anything above 3 is correct for that inequality. The flipping process may work after you are done solving the equation and you figure out the value of the variable.

Representing Time

Time may be represented in an equation in seconds, minutes, hours and so forth. In a question that asks, "How many hours are in 420 minutes?" the student will divide 420 by 60, resulting in 7. This is because seven 60-minute hours equal 420 minutes. Meanwhile, the equation "How many minutes are in one day?" requires a student to multiply 60 x 24 to get 1440.

Time may also be represented with either a 12- or 24-hour time period. The 12-hour time period involves Meridian or

Post Meridian (a.m. and p.m.) hours with no zero hours used. The 24-hour time period, also known as military time, involves the first hour of the day being the zero hour or 0:00. The time will move from 0:00 to 23:59 throughout the day. Therefore, 5:35 PM for a 12-hour clock would be 17:35 on a 24-hour clock.

Basic math equations may be incorporated in time measurements. 25 seconds may be multiplied by 3 to get 75 seconds, or 1 minute and 15 seconds. Since time measurements are based on 24-hour, 60-minute and 60-second intervals, it's vital for students to take careful note of how the equation is set up. If a student adds 1 day and 3 hours to 7:30 p.m. Monday, the student will get 10:30 p.m. Tuesday.

Division may be used in some time-based measurements, although it's used more often to calculate speed or distance. An example would be a car traveling 350 miles over the course of 5 hours and 45 minutes. In this situation, the 45 minutes is added to the 300 minutes from those 5 hours to get 345 total minutes. The 350 miles are divided by the 345 minutes to get a total of the driver traveling 1.014 miles per minute. Another option is to divide 45 by 60 to get 0.75, totaling 5.75 hours. 350 is divided by that total to find that the car went 60.8695 miles per hour during that time.

When representing time based on hours or minutes, you should avoid usually using decimals. For instance, instead of saying 6.5 hours, you can say 6 hours and 30 minutes. And 50.2 minutes would equal 50 minutes and 12 seconds. You may use decimals when you need to include seconds in a calculation. An example would be "The sprinter ran 100 yards in 10.92 seconds." Aim to keep the decimal in the tenths or hundredths. Decimals may be used if you have longer time periods to work with. You may say "18.2 years" instead of "18 years, 2 months and 13 days."

Avoid using shorter measurements of time if a larger measurement is good enough. You might state "3,567 days" in a measurement, but it would be easier to write "9.77 years" instead of that. Similarly, if you're measuring hours and minutes, breaking the number of hours down into days is easier to work with. For instance, "210 hours" would be better listed as "8 days and 18 hours" as this is easier to use in a calculation.

When calculating time based on months, you may use 30 days for the measurement. That is, 2.5 months can be listed as 2 months and 15 days. However, you must use the proper measurements for when specific months are mentioned. This includes using 31 days for January, March, May, July, August, October and December. You'll also use 28 or 29 days for February depending on whether a leap year is involved; 29 days would be used for the leap year, or a year that could be divided by 4.

Representing Money

Money is represented in a decimal form in most cases. The calculations used in money-related math problems focus on both integers and smaller decimals. For instance, money can be listed as $45, $25.56, £8.56 or €5,500 among many other possibilities. The number is rounded to the nearest hundredth every time. Also, a comma will divide the thousands digit from the hundreds digit, the millions digit from the hundred thousands digit, and so forth.

Some monetary calculations might require an answer in the thousandths or lower. In this case, the number may be rounded to a certain total. In most cases, the number must be rounded up to the nearest hundredth. $26.5694 would be changed to $26.57, for example. Many retailers will round up their totals to the nearest cent in such cases; $29.35342 may be closer to $29.35, but that total may still be rounded up to $29.36. In other cases, the number may be rounded to the nearest one or tenth depending on the requirements in an equation.

Converting Measures

In some cases, you will have to convert from one measurement to another. For example, when measuring the length of an item, you might have to convert the number of inches to the number of feet. An example is, "How many inches are in 6 feet?" Since one foot equals 12 inches, the answer would be 72.

To convert between measures, a student needs to look at the measurements in an equation and then identify their values. When an hour is listed, the student will recall that there are 60 minutes in that hour and then another 60 seconds in each minute. For distances, the student will notice that one foot equals 12 inches or that one yard equals 3 feet. The following totals should be utilized by students when converting from one measure to another:

- 16 ounces = 1 pound
- 1 foot = 12 inches
- 1 yard = 3 feet

- 1 mile = 5,280 feet or 1,760 yards
- 1 tablespoon = 3 teaspoons
- 1 fluid ounce = 2 tablespoons
- 1 cup = 8 fluid ounces
- 1 pint = 2 cups
- 1 quart = 2 pints
- 1 gallon = 4 quarts
- 1 barrel = 31.5 gallons

For example, a student may be presented with this problem: "A car can hold 13.5 gallons of fuel in its engine. How many pints does this equal?" The calculation is 13.5 multiplied by 4 to get 54 quarts. The student then multiplies that by 2 to get 108 pints, which is the correct answer. The process of converting between measurements requires having equivalents memorized.

Metric System

Different types of units and measures are used in many parts of the world. The metric system is used almost everywhere except the United States. Whereas people in the United States obey speed limits based on the number of miles per hour they drive, people in Canada and Mexico follow such limits based on the kilometers per hour.

Therefore, you might need to convert the basic American measurements into metric units. This includes using meter and grams, the basic forms of measurement in an equation.

A meter is a distance of length, which is equal to about 3.28 feet. A gram is equal to around 0.035 ounces and a liter, which is about 0.264 gallons.

The numbers in the metric system use certain prefixes. A prefix designates the general value of a number. For example, the prefix kilo- refers to 1,000. Therefore, a kilogram is 1,000 grams in weight.

Metric System Prefixes

The prefixes for numbers move up in the millions on the metric system.

- Mega refers to one million. A megagram is 1,000 kilograms or 1,000,000 grams.

- Giga is one billion. A gigagram is 1,000 megagrams or 1 billion grams.

- Tera is one trillion. A teragram is 1 trillion grams, 1,000 gigagrams or 1 million megagrams in weight.

Some common measurements that are less than 1 in value have individual prefixes as well.

- Deci- is the prefix for one-tenth. 1 decimeter is 0.1 meters in length, or 1 decigram is one-tenth of a gram.

- Centi- stands for hundredths.

- Milli- stands for thousandths. 10 millimeters would equal 1 centimeter, which equals 0.01 meters or 0.1 decimeters.

- The micro-, nano- and pico- prefixes indicate the millionth, billionth and trillionth places, respectively. A picometer is one-trillionth of a meter, for example.

Geometry

Geometry is the study of shapes and measurements. This includes looking at lengths and angles. Geometric equations can involve spatial equations and may be relevant to everyday activities. This test section focuses on helping students identify different aspects of geometry and the rules that govern area and volume of shapes.

Shapes

A geometric shape involves a figure with a boundary within which points, lines and curves may be contained. Some shapes require multiple lines, but a circle or ellipse may also be formed with only one line. The shape can be three-dimensional if several planes are used in its creation.

Polygons

A polygon is a shape that has many sides. A regular polygon has sides that are all the same length. Irregular polygons have sides with different lengths.

The number of sides a polygon has is equal to the number of angles inside the polygon. A square has 4 sides and 4 angles; a hexagon has 6 sides and 6 inside angles; a pentagon has 5 sides and 5 inside angles.

Simple or Complex?

A simple polygon is a shape that has one boundary. Thus, the sides of the polygon all form one consistent shape. A complex polygon has a boundary that can intersect itself. One or more lines overlap the lines within that boundary. This produces the appearance of two or more shapes that are connected together within the same polygon; these shapes can be of any size or style so long as they both are linked with one another.

For instance, a single line may be used when producing a star shape. A person may also draw multiple lines that intersect each other many times to create a star polygon or a pentagram. The shape will involve multiple shapes; for a pentagram, for example, five triangles are formed with a pentagon in the middle. There are no limits to how many times a complex polygon will have its features intersect with one another.

Angles

All polygons include a series of angles. The number of sides on the polygon is equal to the number of angles. An angle is measured based on the number of degrees that it has. Degrees refers to the distance between the two lines that form the angle. When the degree total is higher, the lines are further apart. The angle is measured by looking at how adjacent lines in a polygon intersect with each other. The angle is measured on the inside of the polygon; this is also called an internal angle because of its location.

A right angle is 90 degrees. The two lines are situated perpendicular to one another. An acute angle is less than 90 degrees. This angle features two lines that are closer together. An obtuse angle is at least 90 degrees and involves the lines being further apart, possibly to where the lines may be on the same plane. The largest possible obtuse angle is 179 degrees, while an acute angle can be 1 degree. A 180-degree angle is actually a straight line.

The measurements of the angles will vary based on the number of sides in the polygon. To calculate this, take the number of polygon sides and subtract that total by 2. Multiply that sum by 180 to get the total sum of the angles formed. A triangle, which has three sides, will have three angles that total 180 degrees. A four-sided rectangle or square will be 360 degrees, a five-sided pentagon is 540 degrees, a six-sided hexagon is 720 degrees and so forth.

Triangle

The triangle is a three-sided polygon. This may be an equilateral triangle where the three angles produced by the shape are the same. The sides of the equilateral triangle are the same length, thus making it a regular polygon. An isosceles triangle has two sides of the same length and therefore two angles of the same value. A right triangle has three lines of different lengths and one of the angles is 90 degrees. A scalene triangle's sides are all different lengths.

Quadrilateral

A quadrilateral is a four-sided polygon. This may be found in a square or rectangular form. For a square, all four lines are of the same length. In a rectangle, two sides are parallel to each other and equal in length, while the other two sides are also parallel to one another and the same length. Regardless of shape, a quadrilateral may contain four right angles. If a quadrilateral slants, it's called a parallelogram and has two matching obtuse and acute angles; each matching angle is diagonally opposite to each other. A parallelogram may be formed as a rectangle or square in a slanting pattern. The shape will include two angles and lines of the same value versus two other sets of angles and lines of the same total. The same can be measured by calculating the base and height. The base is the length from the left-most point on the parallelogram to the right-most point. The height is the space between the shape's top and bottom lines.

Additional Shapes Based on Number of Sides

A shape can be named based on the number of sides it has:

- A pentagon is a five-sided shape
- A hexagon is six-sided
- An octagon is eight-sided
- A decagon is ten-sided.

In most cases, these shapes will have sides of the same length. Irregular polygons may still be formed, although a ten-sided shape might not look like a traditional decagon.

A larger polygon with its number of sides in the tens may be calculated with the suffix -contagon. A 30-sided shape is a triacontagon while an 80-sided shape is an octacontagon. These are rare shapes and nothing you're likely to be tested on or will need to teach your students.

Circles and Circular Measurements

A circle is a round shape that features one closed line. The circle is formed by drawing from one central point and moving the pencil or pen around that point with every part of the circle equidistant from that point. Any round shape with points that are not the same distance to the center is as an oval.

The diameter is the distance across a circle going through the center point. The diameter may be calculated by multiplying half the diameter (the radius) by 2.

The radius is a measurement of a straight line going from the center of the circle to the outside edge. This is half of the diameter. The radius may be used in advanced equations involving other physical measurements pertaining to the area or volume of the circle.

The circumference of the circle is its measurement around. The circumference is a measure of $2\pi r$. A circle with a radius of 6 inches will have a circumference of 37.696 inches.

The ellipse is another shape that is similar to the circle. This shape may also be referred to as an oval. It can be measured by analyzing the distance from the middle of the ellipse to the longest end versus the distance to the shortest end.

Three-Dimensional Shapes

Some shapes are designed with multiple surfaces or faces around the polygon. A rectangular solid is formed by using six surfaces or faces. The six faces may also be of the same size and therefore create a cube.

Three measurements are needed when calculating three-dimensional shape volume and surface area: length, height and width. In some cases, the base and height of the shape will be measured, although that varies based on the specific type of shape. Refer to the next section for additional details.

Convexes

A convex polygon features no angles that point inwards. This is an irregular shape and looks as though it's expanding outward. The convex polygon can have many sides but the internal angles within the convex cannot be any larger than 180 degrees.

Concave

Concave is the opposite of convex. An internal angle within a concave polygon is greater than 180 degrees. The shape may be identified by how the polygon looks like a part of the surface is caving in toward its middle. A crown-shaped polygon is an example of this. The points on the crown create a series of internal angles of at least 180 degrees.

Regular Polygons

A regular polygon has any number of sides where all of the angles are of the same degree. Add up the degrees of the angles and divide that total by the number of sides in that shape. Each of a regular triangle's angles is 60 degrees. A pentagon's angles are each 108 degrees, a hexagon's angles are 120 degrees and so forth.

Polygon Measurements

Area

Area is the number of unit squares an object can contain. In this listing, a is a variable referring to the length of one side of a polygon. b may be used in cases where the lengths in the polygon are different. For other shapes, b and h refer to the base or horizontal length of the shape and the height or vertical line of that same shape. For circles, the r refers to the radius:

- Square = a^2
- Rectangle = ab
- Parallelogram = bh
- Trapezoid = h / 2 (top line + bottom line)
- Circle = πr^2
- Ellipse = π x (longest line from central point) x (shortest line from central point)
- Triangle (1/2) bh

Area can be used to determine floor plans or identify items that may take up a certain amount of physical space. For instance, you may measure the area of a poster versus the area of a wall to figure out if the poster is too large to fit in a certain spot.

Surface Area

The surface area is the area of a three-dimensional shape. This is a reference to how much space the object takes up.

This is not to be confused with the volume of an object, which will be discussed in the next section. The surface area can be measured based on the type of shape. This includes cubes and spheres alike. The area of each side has to be calculated and then totaled. For example, a cube is six-sided. To calculate the surface area, the area of one side is calculated and multiplied by 6 or (a x b) x 6.

You can calculate the surface area of the bed of a truck. Next, you can calculate the surface area of an object to figure out its size. You can compare the measurement with the truck capacity to figure out if whatever you want to put in the truck will fit.

A cube is a three-dimensional square. The surface area is measured by determining the area of each side. The total equation is $6a^2$, meaning that the area of a side is multiplied by 6. A cube with each side 10 inches long will have a surface area of 100 x 6, or 160 square inches.

To correctly calculate volume, area, etc., students need to be able to identify whether a shape is a square, rectangle, triangle, box, sphere, prism or cylinder, for example. After identifying the shape, students can use the appropriate formula to calculate the surface area. Note that prisms are rectangular in size in most cases, although the specific shape of a prism can vary. The lateral area may be measured; this is the area of the sides on a figure. The total area may also be measured by taking the lateral area and adding the areas of the two end sides of the prism together.

To get the lateral area, the length and height of the prism are multiplied. The total area involves the length of the end sides multiplied by 2 and then added to the lateral area measurement. The measurement is not as accurate as it is with a cube. However, the total should be measured according to the overall size of the object.

A sphere, which is a three-dimensional circle, may also be measured to get its surface area. The measure comes from calculating $4\pi r^2$. For a sphere with a radius of 5 inches, the total would be calculated as 25. This is then multiplied by 4 and π, thus producing a surface area of 314.15 square inches.

Volume

Volume is a measurement of the inside of a three-dimensional figure. Volume is needed to calculate how much an object can contain. The following formulas are used to calculate volume:

- Cube = a^3
- Rectangular prism = abc (length, width and height)
- Irregular prism = bh (base of the prism times the height)
- Cylinder = $\pi r^2 h$
- Pyramid = (1/3) x (bh)
- Cone = $(1/3)\pi r^2 h$
- Sphere = $(4/3)\pi r^3$
- Ellipsoid = $(4/3)\pi$ x radius of short distance x radius of long distance x radius of width

Volume determines the capacity of an object. For instance, you may see that a vehicle can handle a certain amount of volume in its trunk. You can measure the volume of a sphere to figure out if it can fit into the trunk and then repeat this for other items you also want to add to the trunk.

Perimeter

The perimeter is the distance around a figure. For a polygon, the length of each side is measured and the sides added together.

For a circle, the perimeter is the circumference and is calculated by the equation $2\pi r$. A circle with a radius of 4 inches would have a circumference of 25.132 inches. This will be further discussed in the section on π.

The perimeter may be used to measure the amount of space that a shape takes up. You can also use this for when you have a larger number of sides on a surface. This includes an octagon that may be difficult to calculate.

Coordinates

A grid for coordinates requires an x-axis and y-axis. The x-axis is a horizontal line and the y-axis is vertical. They're joined where they meet at a 90-degree angle. A central point on the grid is where the two axes meet; this center point is the origin. The two axes will then be labeled with a series of positive and negative values.

A point on the coordinate grid is listed with two numbers. For instance, a point may include the coordinates (5, -1). A student will move to the right of the origin to the 5 value on the x-axis. That person will them move down one below the origin to reach -1 on the y-axis. The process may be repeated for as many points that need to be added to the grid.

Some calculations include finding a place that is in the middle of the two coordinates or determining the length between certain coordinates. Sometimes the coordinate grid may help create shapes of certain lengths. The grid can also be used to determine the positions of those shapes with regards to others.

Parallel and Perpendicular Lines

When doing calculations you may come across parallel and perpendicular lines. Parallel lines may be of different lengths or far apart from each other, but they are on the same plane as one another. The distance between the two left-most points is the same as the distance between the right-most points. You may notice these parallel lines on a square, rectangle or other four-sided polygons. When a line intersects parallel lines, the angles that are formed are diagonally apart from each other and equal in size.

Perpendicular lines occur when two lines intersect each other while forming a right angle. The first line is vertical while the second line is horizontal. You may notice perpendicular lines on a right triangle as those two lines create a right angle where they meet.

The Value of π and its Use in Circular Measurements

The ancient mathematician Archimedes used various shapes within a circle and determined there was a constant in all his measurements. That constant was pi (π), which he calculated to be 22/7 or 3.1415. π may be used when calculating the area of a circle, which is π times the radius squared. The formula is πr^2. The volume of a cylinder is calculated by using $\pi r^2 h$, which is pi times the radius squared times the height of the cylinder.

Most calculators have a π button that automatically enters the value of the constant into an equation. However, you can use 3.14 if you don't have access to a calculator or are looking to simplify the equation.

Intepreting Charts and Graphs

Charts and graphs are frequently used in newspapers and other media to provide readers with information as quickly as possible. This includes summarizing statistical data in a visual form. The goal is to simplify the content that a person is reading. Four types of graphs or charts may be used in math equations.

Bar Graph

The bar graph is used to compare data. Each measurement being compared is measured based on the length of a bar. A longer bar has a greater value than a shorter one.

When reading a bar graph, you must first look at the title. The title will list information on what is being measured. For example, a title might state that the bar graph lists a baseball player's batting average over the past couple of years.

Next, review the axes of the bar graph. The x-axis and y-axis should include separate terms. For the baseball player's example, you will see one axis listing the years that the player has completed. Each year should include one bar. The other axis lists the player's possible batting average. The longer bars indicate the largest values. In this case, you might see a bar from 2005 indicating that the baseball player had a batting average of .276. The bar for 2006 would be smaller as it represents an average of .255. Then you might see a larger bar at 2007 for .295. You can compare all of the bars to see how the player did or didn't improve over the years.

Line Graph

A line graph illustrates things that occur over a period of time. The line is read from left to right. The left-most part of the x-axis is the earliest time period represented on the chart. The right-most part is the end of that time. The y-axis is a measure that varies by each item.

For the baseball player, you would look at how the line graph is arranged by year. You will notice that the line keeps going up and down based on the player's performance. You can use this to see how well the player's performance progressed over the years.

Additional lines may be added to a line graph. This is to compare two variables that are different from one another but related to each other based on the subject being depicted. You may come across a chart in our example that includes the original baseball player and two more lines that cover two other players who competed at the same time. The lines should be different in texture or color. You may see that in 2004 Batter A had an average of .315 and Batter B had an average of .235, but in 2009 Batter A's average was .285 while Batter B's average was .340. This means that Batter B improved upon his play over time while Batter A started to slump.

Pictograph

A pictograph is a chart that lists items with symbols. The chart includes a listing of several items that relate to each other and are linked together by the subject matter. Each item will be represented by several symbols with each symbol reflecting a certain variable. You need to determine what each symbol means.

In one case, you might see a listing of baseball teams and how many home runs those teams hit in the past season. Each team will have a series of baseball-shaped symbols next to its name. In this graph, one baseball is equal to 25 home runs. You may see that Baltimore has 4 baseballs next to its name while Chicago has 5. This means that the team from Baltimore hit 100 home runs while the team from Chicago had 125.

Sometimes a symbol is cut in half or is only partially represented on a line. This means that the total number is less than whatever the symbol is worth. You may see in the example that the baseball team from Houston has 5.5 baseballs. This means that the team hit more than 125 home runs, but fewer than 150. The process of halving or producing fractions for symbols will vary in each chart.

Pie Chart

A pie chart is a circle divided into segments. Each slice is a certain size in comparison with other items on the chart. The pie chart is often utilized to calculate the percentages of something. For instance, a chart could feature a listing of all the players on a baseball team. The slices on that pie chart might represent the number of home runs that each person hit. Each slice is worth a certain number of home runs based on each person.

The pie chart might show that one person hit 32 home runs for a team. That person's segment of the pie chart would therefore be larger than another player who hit 8 home runs. Meanwhile, the size of the segment will be based on the total number of home runs hit by every person represented on the pie chart. If the team had 160 home runs, the player who hit 32 home runs would occupy 20% of the chart. The pie chart produces depicts who hits the most and least home runs on a team. Another example uses a pie chart to show how a person's income is spent. The entire pie represents 100% and each segment represents a portion. For example, 30% could be for food, 30% for rent or housing, 10% for utilities, 20% for car and fuel and 10% representing miscellaneous. A pie chart is like a picture and makes it easy to see relationships.

Identifying Trends on Charts and Graphs

Charts and graphs may depict different trends. Trends show the evolution of something, whether positive or negative. For instance, you might see that the value of something is moving up by a certain rate over time. You might also notice that the rate of growth is consistent throughout the entire chart.

An example of a trend would be a baseball player's batting average. A chart might show that the player had a batting average of .240 in the first year. Then, his average went up in the second year to.260, .275 in the third year and.280 in the fourth. The trend in the graph shows the player's batting average is rising every year. However, the rate of the increase is declining with each year, thus suggesting that the player might be reaching a peak in his performance. The trend should be easy to see when you look at how the line starts to go from a curve to a straight line.

Tables

A table is another graphic representation of data. In this case, the table gathers several variables that are measured with a single parameter. A table will have a series of columns that list different variables. There should also be a title at the top of the table to let you know what to expect in terms of the table's content.

A table might depict how many people live in certain homes in a neighborhood. The first column might have a listing that says "Number of People Living in a House," while the second column says "Percentage of Households." One bar might say that 18% of the households have three people in them, while 35% of the households have four people, 15% have five people and 8% have six or more people. You could be asked a question like "What percentage of homes in the neighborhood have five or more people living in them?" You would add the 15 and 8 from the example above to find that 23% of houses in the neighborhood have five or more people living in them.

Teaching Math Skills in the Classroom

Identify the Need

In your work as a paraprofessional, you will have to teach students to identify the key objectives in questions such as whether a problem requires addition, subtraction, multiplication and division. A question might also require a more complex calculation such as finding the square root, area or volume of a specific shape. Teach students to identify what is being asked in a problem and what is required to solve it.

When solving a problem, students need to consider four things:

1. What is the question asking? Students must be able to identify what type of mathematical calculations should be used to solve a problem.

2. What process should be used to solve the question?

3. What formula could be used to solve the question?

4. Is the answer logical? Was the formula written correctly? Students should always check for errors in computations.

<u>Step by Step</u>

Teaching students to work through the individual steps in a problem is vital to your work as a paraprofessional, starting with assessing a problem and determining a "plan of attack."

For example, you might have an equation, such as (5 + 8) x (6 + 9). Explain to the students that the parts in the parentheses (brackets) should be completed first. You would get 13 x 15 as a result. These two numbers are then multiplied to produce the answer of 195.

Recognize the Context

The context refers to the meaning of the question. This helps students determine what concepts are being discussed so they focus on the appropriate aspects of a problem, i.e., multiplication instead of subtraction.

Help Students Learn What Numbers to Focus on in Calculations

Word problems contain many numbers and are sometimes deliberately designed so students have to figure out what numbers to use in an equation and which to ignore. While teaching, you might use different colors to highlight certain numbers. You can also talk about how specific numbers relate to certain parts of an equation. This includes explaining how those numbers change as the equation is calculated.

Completing the Math Test

When completing the math portion of the ParaPro test, first you will look at how to resolve certain math equations. Second, you will concentrate on the key aspects of completing math questions.

Some questions you complete will involve word problems. Carefully read all the instructions in each problem to determine the objective. Figure out what the question is asking and then recall the formula or procedure needed to solve the problem. You must know the rules that apply to math calculations, such as the rules for multiplication and division of whole numbers, mixed numbers, fractions and decimal numbers. Another area of mathematics you will have to know is geometry, such as the names of various shapes and how to calculate area, volume, perimeter and circumference. You'll also need to know simple algebra including solving for unknown values and computing numbers within brackets.

Math Questions

1. The department store is offering a Black Friday special of 30% off a television set. In July, an employee at the store bought that same set with a 15% employee discount and paid $450. How much would the television set be worth on Black Friday?
    a. $350.54
    b. $365.45
    c. $368.50
    d. $370.59

2. Find the answer to the following equation: x + 16 = 45 + (5 x 16)
    a. 109
    b. 110
    c. 111
    d. 115

Review the following table for Questions 3 and 5:

Hockey Player's Goals Per Season

Year	Goals Scored
2006	8
2007	14
2008	16
2009	33
2010	22
2011	31
2012	10

3. Which year did the hockey player score the second-highest number of goals?
    a. 2008
    b. 2009
    c. 2010
    d. 2011

4. In which period did the player experience the largest decline or increase in the number of goals that he scored in a season?
    a. 2008-2009
    b. 2009-2010
    c. 2010-2011
    d. 2011-2012

5. In terms of the number of goals scored in a season, which is the median?
    a. 10
    b. 14
    c. 16
    d. 22

6. You have to divide a rectangular cake that is 24 inches long, 12 inches wide and 4 inches in height. How many 4-by-4-inch square slices can you cut?

    a. 24

    b. 27

    c. 18

    d. 33

7. What is the area of a circle that has a diameter of 6 inches?

    a. 28.27

    b. 51.35

    c. 80.35

    d. 113.09

8. 4.456 kilograms is equal to how many grams?

    a. 44.56

    b. 445.6

    c. 4,456

    d. 44,560

9. Which number is missing in the following sequence: 14, 17, 22, 29, ___, 49?

    a. 37

    b. 38

    c. 39

    d. 40

10. What is the answer to 5.35×10^3?

    a. 535

    b. 5,350

    c. 53,500

    d. 535,000

11. A right triangle has angles of 40 and 50 degrees. The third angle is how many degrees?

    a. 40

    b. 50

    c. 90

    d. 180

12. A yard would be suitable when you need to measure:

    a. Milk for a recipe

    b. Fertilizer for a yard

    c. Wood planks for a floor

    d. Gas for a car

13. Mary's pudding recipe requires two cups of milk for a single serving. If Mary was to serve eight people, how many quarts of milk would she require?

    a. 2

    b. 3

    c. 4

    d. 5

14. What is the answer to 26 x 24?

    a. 600

    b. 616

    c. 624

    d. 632

15. When you divide 135 by 16, what will be the remainder?

    a. 5

    b. 6

    c. 7

    d. 8

16. When you add two odd numbers together, the answer is always going to be:

    a. Positive

    b. Negative

    c. Odd

    d. Even

17. What is the answer to 4/6 + 8/11?

    a. 1 13/33

    b. 12/17

    c. 1 1/11

    d. 1 14/29

18. Estimate the number 165,345,234 to the nearest hundred thousand.

    a. 165,000,000

    b. 165,300,000

    c. 165,345,000

    d. 165,345,200

19. What is the mean of this sequence: 15, 16, 16, 18, 20, 20, 20, 25? Round your answer to the nearest whole number.

    a. 17

    b. 18

    c. 19

    d. 20

20. Joseph completed his 30-page science project in 15 days. Shirley completed the same project in 12 days. If the two of them worked together on the task, how many days would it take for them to finish the project?

    a. 13

    b. 13.5

    c. 14

    d. 14.5

Answers

1. d. The question requires calculating 85% of $450. Divide 450 by 0.85, which equals $529.41. That would be the original value of the television set. Calculate 30% of $529.41 to determine the deduction of the television set, which equals $158.82. Now reduce $529.41 by $158.82. The Black Friday sale price is $370.59.
2. a. In this question, you will calculate 5 x 16 first to get 80. Add 80 to 45 to 125. Subtract 16 from 125 to get 109. The two segments will equal 125 when x = 109.
3. d. Review the columns to see what they include. Note that in 2009, the player had 33 goals, the most in a year. The second-greatest total was two years later in 2011 when that player scored 31 goals.
4. a. By adding or subtracting the totals between each year, you will get the totals of 6, 2, 17, 11, 9 and 11. The difference of 17 occurs between 2008 and 2009.
5. c. To find the median you should organize the numbers in order from smallest to largest as 8, 10, 14, 16, 22, 31 and 33. The number in the middle of those seven is 16, which is the median.
6. c. The volume of the original rectangular cake you are dividing is 1,152 cubic inches. Calculate this as 24 x 12 x 4 = 1,152. A four-inch square would be four inches long and four inches wide. Since the cake is also four inches high, the volume of the slice is calculated by 4^3 = 64 cubic inches. The next step is to find out how many slices of that volume can be made from the volume of the entire cake. This is calculated by dividing 1,152 by 64 = 18..

7. a. Since the diameter is 6 inches, the radius of the circle is 3 inches. Apply the formula πr^2. The equation is $3.14 \times 3^2 = 28.27$.
8. c. 1 kilogram is equal to 1,000 grams. This requires the decimal point to be moved three places to the right.
9. b. The sequence shows the numbers increasing with an increasing total being added in between each number. That total goes up by 2 in between each number. 3 is added to 14, then 5 is added to 17. 7 is added to 22, and then 9 is added to 29 to get 38. Then add 11 to get 49.
10. b. 10^3 is 10 multiplied by itself three times, which equals 1,000. Multiply that by 5.35 to get 5,350.
11. c. The total of the angles in a triangle should be 180 degrees. A right triangle always has a 90-degree angle, and that angle is not part of the question.
12. c. A yard is a measure of length. The gas and milk options are measures of weight or capacity, while the fertilizer is a measure of area. The wood can be measured based on how long the planks are, thus making the yard a suitable measurement standard.
13. c. Mary would require 16 cups of milk for eight people. Two cups equal a pint, which requires you to calculate $16 \div 2$, which equals 8 pints. Two pints equal a quart, so to change pints to quarts requires a calculation of $8 \div 2$, which equals 4 quarts of milk.
14. c. To calculate 26×24, start by taking 26×4 to equal 104. After that, calculate 26×2 to equal 52 while adding a 0 at the end, as you are working with the tens position first. By adding 520 and 104, you will get the correct answer of 624.

15. c. When you divide 135 by 16, you get 8.4375. Take the 8 and multiply that total by 16 to get 128. Add 7 to that to get 135. In this case, 7 would be the remainder.
16. d. Two odd numbers added together will always equal an even number. If you were to add an odd and an even number, you would also get an odd number.
17. a. Find the common denominator of 4/6 and 8/11. This would be 66, thus producing the fractions 44/66 and 48/66. Add them together to get 92/66. This is simplified to 46/33, which can be written as 1 13/33.
18. b. The numeral that occupies the hundred thousand place is the sixth one. 165,300,000 is the nearest hundred thousand.
19. c. The mean requires the numbers to be added together and then divided by the total number of numbers. In this case, 150 ÷ 8, which equals the mean (average) of 18.75, should be rounded to 19.
20. b. The project is the same length for each student. Therefore, you would just add 12 and 15 together and then divide the total by 2 to get 27/2, which equals 13.5.

Section 4: ParaPro Sample Test

The following section features a series of questions that relate to the ParaPro exam. The exam is divided up into sections based on the topics covered in this guide: writing, reading and mathematics, with an emphasis on both general knowledge and teaching instructional concepts. The questions in this guide will not necessarily appear on the official ParaPro test. They are only designed to be simulations of what you may experience as you complete the test.

The questions in this test are laid out in the same way as the questions on the official test. The questions are multiple choice and include four answers. There is only one correct answer for each question.

The answers to each of the questions in this sample test are included at the end of each section. An explanation of each answer is included. Use this test practice to help you prepare for the official ParaPro test.

Reading Skills

Questions 1-4 relate to the following passage:

The Inner Harbor is a popular part of Baltimore that is a favorite of tourists from around the world. This is a section of the city located near the southern end. The region includes a combination of fun tourist spots with various historic areas.

People can find many historic ships in the Inner Harbor. The USS *Torsk*, a submarine that was the last ship to sink an enemy ship in World War II, is on display. The USCGC *Taney*, a cutter that was the last fighting ship still afloat following the attack on Pearl Harbor, is also here. The USS *Constellation* is a unique sloop that remains the only Civil War ship still afloat. The SS *Wright* container ship is occasionally in the Inner Harbor as well; this is an active-duty logistics support ship.

People can visit various museums around the Inner Harbor, including the Port Discovery children's museum and a museum dedicated to the Civil War. Ripley's Believe It Or Not also has a museum, or "Odditorium," that features unusual artifacts and exhibits. That museum can be identified by the sea monster emerging from the building.

Camden Yards and the M&T Bank Stadium are nearby as well. These are the homes of the Baltimore Orioles baseball club and the Baltimore Orioles football team, respectively. The city's convention center is next to those venues as well.

1. Which of these ships is a submarine?
    a. *Taney*
    b. *Wright*
    c. *Torsk*
    d. *Constellation*
2. If you see a sea monster protruding from a building in the Inner Harbor, that means you are at the:
    a. Food court
    b. Ripley's Believe It or Not Museum
    c. M&T Bank Stadium
    d. Port Discovery
3. The spatial word listed in this passage is:
    a. South
    b. Next to
    c. Around
    d. All of the above
4. What error can be found in the fourth paragraph?
    a. Switching the topic
    b. Unnecessary information
    c. Complicated words
    d. Incorrect syntax

Refer to these sentences for Question 5:

The media hounded a politician about a controversial issue. The reporters wanted answers or more details.

5. *Hounded* in this sentence refers to:
    a. Bothering
    b. Avoiding
    c. Ignoring
    d. Studying

Refer to the following index example for Questions 6 and 7:

Cincinnati, Ohio
    Bridges 34
    Buildings 38-41
    History 54-56, 60
    Sporting venues 58-59
    Theaters 62-63

6. Which of the listings in the index includes data spread over non-consecutive pages?
    a. History
    b. Bridges
    c. Sporting venues
    d. Theaters

7. What page would you choose to find information on baseball and football stadiums in Cincinnati?
    a. 34
    b. 40
    c. 58
    d. 63

Refer to the following passage for Questions 8-11:

The National Hockey League has experienced many changes in its history. Part of this is the league's increase in size to 31 teams. Some teams came from other professional leagues while others came from other cities.

In 1967, the Pittsburgh Penguins and Philadelphia Flyers both entered the league. The Washington Capitals and

Kansas City Scouts joined in 1974. The most recent expansion was in 2017 when the Vegas Golden Knights entered the league.

Other teams entered the league from other hockey leagues. Four teams from the World Hockey Association, which ran from 1972 to 1979, joined the NHL after the league folded. The Edmonton Oilers was one such league.

Many teams also relocated to different cities. The Kansas City Scouts became the New Jersey Devils in the early 1980s. The Quebec Nordiques and Hartford Whalers both relocated in the mid-1990s to become the Colorado Avalanche and Carolina Hurricanes, respectively.

Some teams changed their nicknames over the years. The franchise from Toronto was originally called the Toronto Arenas, but it was renamed the Toronto St. Patricks in 1919 and eventually named the Toronto Maple Leafs in 1927. The Chicago Black Hawks were renamed in the Chicago Blackhawks in the 1980s. The Mighty Ducks of Anaheim became the Anaheim Ducks in the 2000s.

8. Which of these events was the most recent?
    a. Philadelphia Flyers joined the league
    b. Washington Capitals joined the league
    c. The WHA folded
    d. Mighty Ducks of Anaheim changed their name

9. What year could the World Hockey Association have existed?
    a. 1967
    b. 1974
    c. 1985
    d. 1996

10. What is the earliest event listed in the passage?
    a. The Toronto St. Patricks changed their name
    b. The Toronto Arenas changed their name
    c. The Chicago Black Hawks shortened their name
    d. The Quebec Nordiques relocated

11. The main focus within the article involves:
    a. Changes to the league
    b. How teams are formed
    c. Team nickname changes
    d. Team relocations

Refer to this passage for Questions 12-15:

You must act fast to clean a red juice stain spill on the floor. It is easier to remove the stain when it is fresh. The juice will settle into a surface if the compound is not treated quickly.

Remove as much of the juice as possible by blotting the area. Wash the surface with cold water to loosen as much of the juice stain as possible.

A stain remover may be used on the soiled surface. The remover should be applied evenly. Make sure the remover does not contain any discoloring bleach agents.

Vinegar and lemon may be mixed with water to remove the stain. The compounds work by adjusting the pH level of the stain. A brush may be used to further dislodge the stain. After you have attempted to remove the stain, allow the area to dry.

Whatever you do, make sure you only use cold water and/or other compounds as anything hot may set the stain.

12. The directions in this passage show you how to:
    a. Clean surfaces
    b. Boil cold water
    c. Remove a red juice stain
    d. Use vinegar

13. According to the passage, you should do this with water:
    a. Use cold water
    b. Apply it evenly
    c. Spread it with a brush
    d. Repeat the process by adding water many times

14. When can you use a brush?
    a. After applying vinegar and lemon to the stain
    b. While using cold water
    c. When using hot water
    d. When you first notice the stain

15. When using a stain remover, you need to:
    a. Shake before use
    b. Keep it warm
    c. Read the types of stains it treats
    d. Make sure it doesn't contain bleach

Review this sentence for Question 16:

The best present is one that a person will use many times.

16. In this sentence, *present* refers to:
    a. A gift
    b. The current time
    c. Being in an attendance at an event
    d. A presentation

Review this sentence for Question 17:

The worst part of the school day is waiting in the rain for the school bus to arrive.

17. The sentence's main point is:
    a. The school day
    b. The school bus
    c. The experience of a school day
    d. The rain

Refer to this passage for Question 18:

Our general goal is to move forward in the coming school year. We have several bus routes planned and a full lunch schedule ready. We also have plans for after-school activities.

18. The main theme in the passage involves:
    a. Plans for school functions
    b. The coming school year
    c. The school board
    d. Specific activities

Answers

1. c. The *Torsk* is the only ship listed that is a submarine.
2. b. The words "That museum" link to Ripley's Museum in the previous sentence.
3. d. Each of these words is a spatial word. "South" is more specific.
4. a. The fourth paragraph includes information on more than one topic: the sports venues in the area and the convention center. The convention center should be mentioned in another paragraph on its own or with other business-related topics.
5. a. The second sentence states that the reporters want answers from the politician. Therefore, they would bother, or hound, the politician in hopes of getting answers.
6. a. The history is written over four pages, but only three of them are in consecutive order.
7. c. You can turn to either page 58 or 59 when trying to find information on sports venues, although the first page is recommended.
8. d. It took place in the 2000s. The other entries were in the 1960s or 1970s.
9. b. The World Hockey Association was in operation from 1972 to 1979. 1974 is the only possible correct answer.
10. b. The earliest listed event was in 1919 when the Arenas changed their name.
11. a. The changes to the league is an appropriate answer as it includes the other three entries on the list. The passage shows that the league has changed substantially over the years.

12. c. The main point of this passage is how to remove a red juice stain from a surface. The other entries may be applicable, but they are not the main idea.
13. a. The passage says that the water should be cold and hot water must be avoided.
14. a. The brush should be used after vinegar and lemon are applied.
15. d. The article says that the stain remover may contain bleaching agents and that you should avoid anything that contains compounds that might discolor a surface.
16. a. The word "present" in this sentence refers to a person receiving a gift that someone will enjoy.
17. c. The content in the sentence indicates the worst thing that could happen during the day. Therefore, the main idea involves rain.
18. a. Although the passage doesn't list any specifics, it includes information about the functions the school will plan in the coming year.

Reading Skills

1. The main difference between skimming and scanning is:
    a. The type of content found
    b. The speed at which these are done
    c. How much content is reviewed at a time

2. When reviewing the author's intention in a passage, you have to look at:
    a. The author's personal history or experience
    b. The author's background
    c. Why that author is writing
    d. All of the above

3. Which of the following signal words may be used to identify the cause and effect relationship between items?
    a. Likewise
    b. First
    c. Last
    d. Because of

4. When can a dictionary be used?
    a. When you need the definition of a word
    b. To review word tenses
    c. To determine the category of a word
    d. All of the above

5. An agree/disagree statement requires the student to:
    a. Explain the content in a passage
    b. Identify connections in the work with other readings
    c. Express one's feelings before and after reading a passage
    d. Determine the author's background or attitudes

6. A hypothesis' purpose is:
    a. To predict
    b. To conclude
    c. To confirm
    d. To analyze

7. When a writer uses many synonyms in one paragraph, the writer is:
    a. Expanding word content
    b. Describing details
    c. Emphasizing a certain point
    d. Focusing on a scene

8. A long vowel sound is most often produced when:
    a. 2 vowels are written together
    b. 2 of the same vowel are next to each other
    c. A vowel takes up an entire syllable
    d. A vowel is louder

9. In the word "proactively," "active" is the:
    a. Root word
    b. Prefix
    c. Suffix
    d. Compound

10. A compound word requires the reader to:
    a. Divide a word into two halves or parts
    b. Count the number of syllables in a compound word
    c. Combine two words together to create a new word
    d. See how the word is used in context with the rest of the sentence

11. Skimming is different from completing a flyover in that skimming concentrates on finding:
    a. The background
    b. The main idea
    c. Specific details
    d. Excess data

12. An emotional word is designed to focus on:
    a. What a writer truly feels about a subject
    b. How people feel about certain things in a situation
    c. The attitudes that large groups hold
    d. All of the above

Answers

1. a. While skimming involves looking for various main concepts and ideas, scanning focuses on an extremely specific type of content. This may include a singular topic.
2. d. Each of these points may be used to identify the author's actions. An author with experience in the field and a strong background may be particularly trustworthy.
3. d. The words "Because of" refer to how an effect occurs because of a certain cause.
4. d. A dictionary may be used for all of these purposes. A dictionary entry should include information on how a word can be utilized and whether there are any significant changes in the tenses.
5. c. Before reading, a student will state if he or she agrees or disagrees with specific concepts. After reading, the student will provide details on whether his or her opinion changed.
6. a. A hypothesis is designed to predict what may happen.
7. c. A sentence that includes multiple synonyms places a focus on a certain item or concept. This includes focusing on a certain attribute relating to the content.
8. a. when 2 vowels are written together in a word, the vowel sound is most often a long vowel, such as ai, ei, oa, ee.
9. a. The root of a word can be found by deleting the prefix and/or suffix. In the word proactively, "active" is the root word, "pro-" is the prefix and "-ly" is the suffix.

10. c. A compound word involves two words that are combined to create another word. An example is "handle" and "bar" being combined to form "handlebar." The definition of the new word may be different from the two words that were combined.
11. b. Skimming allows the reader to find the main idea of a passage. A flyover is a quick review of the content in general while finding as many details on the content as possible.
12. d. All of these answers are correct. A person who writes in the first person may express their own emotions. Emotional words can express individual and group-based feelings.

Writing Questions

1. What word is required in the blank? "Have you seen the new shopping mall? ___ very appealing."

    a. It's

    b. Its

    c. Is

    d. Its'

2. What is the proper plural form of *channel*?

    a. Channels

    b. Channeles

    c. Channles

    d. None of the above

3. What is the error in this sentence? "The boy looked at the neighbor's truck and sit in the passenger seat."

    a. Improper reference

    b. Wrong apostrophe

    c. Improper order of words

    d. Wrong verb agreement

4. What is the correct spelling of the synonym of "tasty"?

    a. Dedicious

    b. Delicious

    c. Delicous

    d. Delecious

5. What part of this sentence is incorrect? "The Smiths and Fox's were waiting for their dinner tables at the restaurant."

    a. Smiths

    b. Fox's

    c. waiting

    d. at the restaurant

6. What is the error in this sentence? "Playing football, studying science, and to exercise were among Janet's favorite hobbies while in high school."

    a. and to exercise

    b. Janet's

    c. hobbies while

    d. in high school

7. What is the incorrect word in this sentence? "Mr. Smith was criticized by people for being the only man which wanted to demolish the building."

    a. criticized

    b. only

    c. which

    d. demolish

8. Which of the words in this sentence is an adverb? "The doctor was effectively helping her patients to feel better."

    a. doctor

    b. effectively

    c. helping

    d. better

9. Where is a comma needed in this sentence? "Since the team was undefeated it would be easy for them to get into the playoffs to compete even further."

    a. undefeated, it

    b. easy, for

    c. playoffs, to

    d. compete, even

10. Correct this sentence: "I reviewed the library's catalogue, but they did not have the books that I wanted."

    a. Move the apostrophe in library's to the end

    b. Replace "they" with "it"

    c. Replace "want" with "wanted"

    d. Change the comma to an apostrophe

11. Which is an example of a form of parallelism?

    a. Troy enjoys kicking footballs and to shoot hockey pucks.

    b. Troy enjoys to kick footballs and shooting hockey pucks.

    c. Troy enjoys kicking footballs and shooting hockey pucks.

    d. Troy wants to kick footballs while shooting hockey pucks.

12. Which of these sentences illustrates an appropriate agreement?

    a. All the dogs is ready for their walking session.

    b. All the dogs are ready for its walking session.

    c. All the dogs is ready for its walking session.

    d. All the dogs are ready for their walking session.

Refer to the following passage for Questions 13-14:

Jerry was looking in the window of the science lab. He saw various objects on the table including a few vials of multicolored fluids. However, Jerry did not have much time to look around. He walked away from the window. He did not tell anyone about what he saw.

13. What point of view is this passage being told in?

    a. First person

    b. Second person

    c. Third person

    d. Third person omnipresent

14. Which of the following verbs can also be a noun?

    a. Looking

    b. Saw

    c. Walked

    d. Tell

15. A semicolon could be added between:

    a. First and second sentences

    b. Second and third sentences

    c. Third and fourth sentences

    d. Fourth and fifth sentences

16. Identify the noun in this sentence: "The best part of the meal was the dessert with the whipped cream on top."

    a. meal

    b. dessert

    c. whipped cream

    d. All of the above

17. Identify the verb(s): "The walk was enjoyable, especially when the couple ran across the field."

    a. walk, ran

    b. couple

    c. was, ran

    d. across, field

18. Identify the adjective: "Young Travis was mad about how the football game ended."

    a. Travis

    b. young

    c. game

    d. ended

Answers

1. a. *It's* is the only logical option. The apostrophe emphasizes how the word refers to a certain action.
2. a. The first option is the correct spelling for the word.
3. a. The verb "looked" is past tense and the other verb has to agree. "Sit" should be "sat."
4. b. "Delicious" is the only correct spelling.
5. b. The last name "Fox" is written incorrectly as a plural possession. The word "Foxes" could be used instead.
6. a. The activities need to agree. Replace "and to exercise" with "exercising."
7. c. The word "who" should be used instead of "which," as "who" directly links up to Mr. Smith in this case.
8. b. "Effectively" is an adverb in this sentence. The "doctor" is a noun, "helping" is a verb, and "better" is an adjective.
9. a. The adverb clause at the beginning of the sentence should have a comma at the end to link that clause to the next point that needs to be discussed.
10. b. The word "library" is a singular word and therefore does not need a plural pronoun. The sentence illustrates a disagreement between the noun and pronoun. Replacing "they" with "it" is necessary for fixing the issue, thus creating an agreement.
11. c. Parallelism involves the items that link with each other in a sentence using the same grammatical form. In this case, "kicking" and "shooting" are in

the same form. The other three sentences are not grammatically correct.
12. d. This is the only answer where the pronouns are in the plural form. The sentence focuses on the dogs being identical.
13. c. The narrative is told in the third person. This is not an omnipresent third person form because the narrator does not know what the character is thinking. The narrator is only mentioning what can be seen.
14. c. "Walk" could be used as a noun to explain a physical activity, as in 'went for a walk.' It could also be a length of cement leading to a door, as in 'the walk' was lined with flowers.
15. d. A semicolon may be used in cases where the sentences are linked to each other with some form of immediacy. The fourth and fifth sentences are the best ones to add a semicolon between. A semicolon is unnecessary for the other sentences in the passage.
16. d. Each of the choices can be seen as a noun. The meal concentrates on the basic topic of the sentence, while the dessert and the whipped cream are added details.
17. c. "Walk" is used as a noun in this situation. "Was" and "ran" are the verbs in the sentence.
18. b. "Young" is the adjective as it modifies "Travis."

Writing Skills Questions

1. What should you avoid doing as you write a conclusion?

    a. Adding new details

    b. Repeating ideas

    c. Addressing future ideas

    d. All of the above

2. When is it best to add an anecdote to your writing?

    a. During the introduction

    b. Halfway through an essay

    c. In the conclusion

    d. Avoid anecdotes if possible

3. The warrant in an argument focuses on:

    a. The key part of an argument

    b. The general claim

    c. Special considerations for an argument

    d. Identifying all sides of the argument

4. Bias may be shown when:

    a. Evidence of a subject is presented

    b. No proper evidence is shown

    c. A person avoids assumptions

    d. The writer is being sympathetic toward one party or side

5. How long should the conclusion be in a piece of writing?

    a. A few paragraphs

    b. Several pages

    c. Two or three pages

    d. As long as the writer needs it to be

6. What is the greatest risk involved with using the word "it" in a sentence?

    a. Being vague

    b. Being direct

    c. Simplifying the subject matter

    d. Making the writing too simple

7. Active voice differs from passive voice in that active voice:

    a. Directly explains a subject's action

    b. Involves multiple subjects

    c. Concentrates on what may happen in the future

    d. Has to be in the past tense

8. When is it okay to write a long sentence?

    a. It's generally acceptable

    b. A few times here and there

    c. As seldom as possible

    d. Never

9. Words like before, first and later are what types of transition words?

    a. Example

    b. Exception

    c. Sequential

    d. Similarity

10. An adverb will explain all of the following about a verb except:

    a. How

    b. Why

    c. Where

    d. When

11. The thesis statement is designed to discuss:

    a. The general topic that will be presented in the writing

    b. A prediction of what may happen in the writing

    c. Summarize the writing

    d. An abstract

12. An addition transition may include words like:

    a. Likewise

    b. After

    c. Also

    d. Besides

Answers

1. d. The conclusion is designed to be a summary, but not to introduce any new ideas.

2. a. An anecdote may be used in the introduction. The story may pique readers' interest to continue reading.

3. b. A warrant can be used to focus on the general argument being made.

4. b. Bias is shown by a writer when the writer indicates an obvious preference for one subject or side of an argument.

5. a. The conclusion should be concise. A few paragraphs should be enough.

6. a. The word "it" is vague and might mean various things unless the subject is explained in the sentence or the sentence prior.

7. a. The active voice indicates the direct action of a subject.

8. c. There may be cases where a long sentence is permissible. If the long sentence could be two complete sentences, a semicolon is used between the two. However, a person should avoid using long sentences if possible to keep the work from being too complicated or hard to read.

9. c. The words all refer to specific actions that may take place within a certain order and are sequential transition words.

10. b. The adverb doesn't explain why a verb action took place.

11. a. The thesis focuses on describing the topic to be discussed without explaining it. It does not predict what the writer will discuss; a hypothesis is a prediction.

12. c. "Also" is the only word that could be used as an addition transition word. The word suggests that something is to be included.

Math Questions

1. The water bill in the house costs 35 cents for each gallon of water used. Tom used 1,500 gallons of water in June, 1,700 gallons in July and 1,400 gallons in August. What is the average value of Tom's water bill?

    a. $512.55

    b. $536.67

    c. $541.58

    d. $560.79

2. A road map shows that 1 inch is equal to 20 miles. The spacing between the driver's home and the destination is about 3 1/3 inches. Therefore, the distance from the driver's home and the destination is approximately how many miles?

    a. 55.55

    b. 66.66

    c. 77.77

    d. 80

3. What would 3 1/6 be when you convert it to an irregular fraction?

    a. 4/6

    b. 3/18

    c. 3/6

    d. 19/6

Review the following table for Questions 4-6:

Year-End Total of Widgets Sold By Retail Location (in thousands)

Year	Cleveland	Columbus	Cincinnati
2010	17	22	18
2011	14	22	16
2012	10	23	13
2013	8	25	12
2014	11	26	12
2015	19	26	11

4. Which region experienced the largest growth or decline in the number of widgets sold from one year to the next?

    a. Cleveland

    b. Columbus

    c. Cincinnati

    d. All three are equal

5. The sales of widgets in Cincinnati have declined by the following percentage from 2012 to 2015:

    a. 13.5

    b. 15.4

    c. 16.6

    d. 17.2

6. Which city has the second-largest mean?

    a. Cleveland

    b. Columbus

    c. Cincinnati

    d. Cleveland and Cincinnati are tied

7. If $8x = 48$, then $5 + x =$

    a. 10

    b. 11

    c. 12

    d. 13

8. The upper-left corner of a parallelogram has an angle of 35 degrees. The lower-right or upper-right corner of that same polygon has an angle of:

   a. 55

   b. 85

   c. 115

   d. 145

9. George wants to covert his American dollars into Canadian dollars. The current exchange rate is 1 American dollar equals 1.25 Canadian dollars. How many American dollars will George need to exchange in order to get $400 in Canadian currency?

   a. 300

   b. 320

   c. 350

   d. 375

10. Compute the following equation: $14 + (4 \times 5^2)$

    a. 114

    b. 34

    c. 200

    d. 450

11. Complete the following sequence: 3, 5, 6, 8, 9, 11, 12, ___

    a. 13

    b. 14

    c. 15

    d. 16

12. Which of these is not an appropriate answer for x in the equation $4 + x \leq 10$?

    a. 4

    b. 5

    c. 6

    d. 7

13. The length of a triangle from its left-most point to its right-most point is 4.5 inches. The height of that triangle from top to bottom is 3.5 inches. What is the area of that triangle in square inches?

    a. 7.875

    b. 8.275

    c. 12.25

    d. 15.75

14. A portable flash drive can handle about 8 gigabytes of data. Michael needs to copy an installation file that is 600 megabytes to a flash drive. That file will take up this much of the flash drive's capacity:

    a. 7.5%

    b. 8%

    c. 8.5%

    d. 10%

15. Line A is a straight line. Line B intersects that line to create four angles. The angle on the top left is 48 degrees. What is the size of the angle at the bottom right?

    a. 42

    b. 48

    c. 62

    d. 132

16. Calculate 45 + (34 − 15) + 16.

    a. 80

    b. 90

    c. 95

    d. 100

17. An endurance racing team is taking part in a 12-hour race. The team has two drivers, Greg and Mark. The team plans to have Greg drive 55% of the race while Mark will drive the other 45%. What is the amount of time Greg will spend driving?

    a. 6 hours 30 minutes

    b. 6 hours 36 minutes

    c. 6 hours 42 minutes

    d. 7 hours

18. Sandy is trying to calculate her GPA for the past year. She took a two-hour course and got a B, a three-hour course that resulted in an A, another three-hour course with a C and a four-hour course with a B. Classes that have more hours factor into the GPA more than shorter ones. Assuming that the GPA is determined based on the letter grade (A=4, B=3, C=2, D=1, F=0), what is Sandy's GPA to the nearest hundredth?

    a. 2.85

    b. 3.00

    c. 3.15

    d. 3.33

Answers

1. b. You would take each of the three monthly totals and add them together to get a total of 4,600 gallons. 35 cents is represented as 0.35. Multiply 4,600 by 0.35 and you will get a total of $1,610. Divide the total by 3 to get $536.6666. Since this is currency, you have to round the total to the nearest hundredth. The final answer is $536.67.
2. b. Converting 3 1/3 to an improper fraction equals 10/3. Then 20 is converted to 20/1. Multiply 10/3 x 20/1 equals 200/3. This gives you a total of 66.66 miles.
3. d. 3 would be 6/6 three times over, thus producing 18/6. Add that to 1/6 to equal 19/6, which is the irregular fraction.
4. a. From 2014 to 2015, the number of widgets sold in Cleveland increased by 8,000, thus making it the largest year-to-year increase or decrease listed on the map.
5. b. The number of widgets sold in Cincinnati dropped from 13,000 to 11,000 during that time period. By dividing 11,000 by 13,000, you will get 0.846. This may be reversed to 0.154, which is then converted to 15.4%. Therefore, there was a 15.4% drop in widget sales in Cincinnati from 2012 to 2015.
6. c. Columbus has the largest mean total of 24,000 widgets. Cleveland had a mean of 13,166, and Cincinnati had a mean of 13,666. Cincinnati has the second-largest mean.
7. b. Divide 48 by 8 to find x. 6 = x. Use 6 in the next equation to arrive at a sum of 11.

8. d. Since the first angle is 35 degrees, the other angle must equal 145 degrees to complete 180 degrees.
9. b. Divide the Canadian currency by 1.25, which equals $320 in US currency.
10. a. The question requires the calculations to be done in a certain order. First, 5^2 = 25. Then multiply 25 x 4 = 100. Finally, add the 100 + 14 =114.
11. b. The sequence shows 2 is added to a number and then 1 to the next number and then 2 to the number after that, so the cycle repeats. At this point in the sequence, you will add 2 + 12 =14.
12. d. The ≤ states that x + 4 is less than or equal to 10. Therefore, x can be worth as much as 6. If a < were to be used, only 4 or 5 would be the correct answers.
13. a. The area of a triangle is calculated by applying the formula ½ bh, which would be ½ x (4.5 x 3.5). The numbers in the brackets are calculated first 4.5 x 3.5 = 5.75. That number is then multiplied by ½ or divided by 2. The result is 7.875 square inches.
14. a. 8 gigabytes equals 8,000 megabytes. Divide 600 by 8,000 to get 0.075, which equals 7.5%.
15. b. The four angles are 2 angles of 48 degrees and 2 angles of 132 degrees. The diagonal sizes are the same. Therefore, the top-left and bottom-right angles are 48 degrees, and the top-right and bottom-left angles are each 132 degrees.
16. a. The part in brackets is calculated first. 34 - 15 = 9. The three numbers added together equal 80.
17. b. 12 hours equals 60 minutes, which means the race will last for 720 minutes. Then 720 is multiplied by 0.55 to equal 396 minutes. To express this in hours, calculate 396 minutes ÷ 60 minutes. This equals 6 hours with 36 minutes left over.

18. b. This is a weighted average question. Calculate 2 x 3, 3 x 4, 3 x 2 and 4 x 3 separately to equal 6, 12, 6 and 12. Add the numbers together to equal 36. Then, divide 36 by 12 hours to equal 3 hours. The GPA is 3.00.

Math Application Questions

1. In the metric system, which prefix represents the largest amount?

    a. Kilo-

    b. Mega-

    c. Giga-

    d. Tera-

2. What is the total value of the angles in the hexagon?

    a. 360

    b. 540

    c. 720

    d. 900

3. Which of these shapes does not qualify as a quadrilateral?

    a. Trapezoid

    b. Parallelogram

    c. Square

    d. Ellipse

4. Which measurement is used first when solving a math problem?

    a. Subtraction

    b. Multiplication

    c. Anything inside a parenthesis or brackets

    d. Exponent

5. Which measure of π is recommended to be used?

    a. 3.1

    b. 3.14

    c. 3.1415

    d. 3.141592

6. What type of variable works best when creating a line graph?

    a. Location

    b. Object

    c. Time

    d. All of the above

7. Estimation can be used in math to move numbers to:

    a. A certain whole number

    b. A specific decimal point

    c. A fraction

    d. A and B

8. When working with money, how should you round the numbers?

    a. To the nearest hundredth

    b. To the nearest tenth

    c. To the nearest one

    d. To the nearest thousandth

9. Which of these measures is largest in size?

    a. Gallon

    b. Barrel

    c. Pint

    d. Quart

10. The surface area is used to measure:

    a. The amount of space that the object occupies in a physical environment

    b. The floor or wall space

    c. The volume inside of the shape

    d. The diameter of the shape

11. The following shape's volume is calculated by squaring the radius of the object and multiplying that total by its height and π ($\pi r^2 h$):

    a. Cylinder

    b. Cone

    c. Sphere

    d. Ellipsoid

12. What is the first thing you should notice when looking at a chart or graph?

    a. The variable

    b. The duration of the chart

    c. The title

    d. The number of items being measured

Answers

1. d. Tera- means one trillion of something. A terabyte is one trillion bytes. Giga- means one billion, mega- means one million and kilo- is one thousand.
2. c. The total is calculated as 180 x 4 =720. The 4 is the result of 6 - 2.
3. d. A quadrilateral is a four-sided shape. Since an ellipse is closer to a circle and doesn't have sides, that shape is not considered a quadrilateral.
4. d. You can use estimation to round a whole number or a decimal number. Fractions are very specific and can be simplified.
5. d. The number with the exponent is solved first, followed by anything in parentheses or brackets, then addition, multiplication and finally subtraction and division.
6. b. 3.14 is the best option for simplified calculations.
7. c. A line graph works best when explaining things that take place over a period of time. A bar graph can be used for any of the options.
8. a. Since a majority of countries divide their monetary units into hundredths, you should narrow your answers to the nearest hundredth.
9. b. A barrel is 31.5 gallons. A gallon is 4 quarts, and a quart is 2 pints.
10. a. The surface area is used on three-dimensional shapes to identify how much space an item may take up. This is different from the area, as that would focus on the space that an item occupies on a flat surface.
11. a. The cylinder and cone are the only two objects on the list that can have volumes calculated. The

volume of a cylinder is calculated with the formula $\pi r^2 h$ and the volume of a cone is calculated with the formula $1/3 \pi r^2$

12. c. By looking at the title, you can determine what a chart or graph is depicting.

Section 5: Additional Details

The following sections provide additional information to assist you when taking the test.

Completing the Test

The information you will come across on the ParaPro test is critical to your success in becoming a paraprofessional. You can use this information to help you complete the test within the amount of time that you are allotted. This information may also be shared with students to help them understand what they can do when taking tests themselves.

<u>Managing Choices</u>

Throughout the test, you will be asked to answer a question based on a series of choices. You must review each choice alongside the question to get a clear idea of what the question is asking of you. As you review the choices, focus on the ones that you know are closer to the correct answer. You may also eliminate anything that you know is incorrect. For instance, you might have the question:

Which word is the noun in this sentence? "Sharon quickly went shopping."

   a. Sharon
   b. Quickly
   c. Went
   d. Shopping

In this case, you might know that "quickly" is not a noun, thus allowing you to immediately rule that out. You will then focus on the other three choices. You can review each word to figure out if it meets the requirements for being a noun. After further review, you will determine that Sharon is the only choice that could be a noun. Therefore, A would be the correct answer.

You can also substitute your answer to the question if possible. You might see a question that reads "15 x _ = 75." You can substitute 5 for that variable to see that by multiplying that with 15, you would get 75. Substituting your answer helps you to visualize the question. This gives you a clearer idea of whether or not a statement is accurate.

Review the Question Wording

The words used in the question will help you quickly determine the objective. The wording may list specific criteria for what you need to do when answering a question. You might be told to answer a question in a specific way. The information in the wording will help you adjust your plans for answering the question. For instance, you may notice the following words in a question:

- Which of the following
- Not
- The most/highest/greatest
- The least/fewest
- Except

For instance, a question may ask, "Which if these concepts are not included in this passage?" The "not" lets you know that you have to identify what point is not featured in whatever you might have just read. That question may also be rephrased as, "All of these concepts are highlighted in the reading except___:"

Questions on Visual Data or Readings

You may be asked questions on how to identify what is represented by a visual chart or table. In other cases, you will need to answer a question related to a specific reading. A good rule of thumb is to read the question or questions relating to that content before you look at the passage or the chart. By reviewing the questions first, you will understand what you need to look for when reviewing the visual content. You can use the information in a question to determine key ideas in a reading passage or to comprehend what the chart or graph you are reading involves.

Applying to Take a **ParaPro** *Test*

You can register for the ParaPro test directly through a testing center. The ETS website can assist you in the process of applying for the test. To complete the process, visit the official ETS website to find the nearest test center. The ParaPro test is conducted throughout the year at various centers around the country.

You can find information on the nearest testing center by visiting https://www.ets.org/parapro/register/. The site includes information on registering for the test. The site lists all of the testing centers by state, with many states having multiple testing centers. Be advised that you might have to travel a long distance as not all states have testing centers that can support the ParaPro test.

After you select the test center where you wish to complete the test, you can contact that center. You will then be given multiple options to consider as to the time that you can take your test. There are multiple times each month when tests are scheduled. Be sure to choose a time that fits your schedule and your ability to travel to the location where the test is to be conducted.

Sending Test Results

You will have to specify a recipient for your test score results. Your application should include a code that details where your test will be sent. This is to ensure that the proper school will receive the test results. You can visit https://www.ets.org/parapro/register/codes/ to find a full listing of the codes of various schools. Each school will be listed by state, the name of the school district or county and the district number associated with that school.

Some school districts or states may not have the proper codes. These are districts or states that use different standards for accepting paraprofessionals. You will have to contact those schools individually to get information on what they require. Fortunately, a majority of schools around the United States accept the test.

Test Day

You must provide proper proof of identification at the center where you will be taking your test. The identification may include not only your identification card like a driver's license but also biometric identification, such as a voice print or fingerprint. The requirements may vary based on the testing center you visit. You must participate in any biometric activities that are required. Failure to provide the required proof of identification will prevent you from taking the test.

You will be required to remove any electronic devices. You are not allowed to use a calculator or anything else that might assist you in the test-taking process. You may also be told to remove your watch if you have one. You should be able to see a clock on the wall to let you know how much time you have left to complete the test.

In most centers, you will complete the test using a computer. A computerized test will make it easier for your scores to be sent to an appropriate center. Also, the computerized test will use randomized questions. In some cases, a test will be provided in paper form.

Scoring

The unofficial score of your test will be displayed after you have finished the test. The official score will be based on further analysis and to confirm your ability to complete the test. The official totals should be available about two to three weeks after you have completed the test. The test will be sent to the school district that bought the assessment you have taken. Your score may also be sent to a teaching certification office in your state, although that could vary. You can also visit https://www.ets.org/parapro/scores/add_scores/ to learn more about how to get a separate score report if you need to send it to another institution. This service will require additional payment.

The scoring should include information on how well you completed the questions in all the segments in the test. However, ETS does not offer information on how much value is placed on each question. Rather, your grade will be determined using the three main segments of the test. You may use this to understand your strengths and whether you need to improve in a certain area. This is particularly critical if you did not meet the required score and need extra study.

The raw score is also included. This value refers to the number of questions that you answered correctly on the test. The value of each question is hidden, although you will get a general score next to the raw value. In some cases, the questions you answered correctly might have been worth more than others due to how difficult or complicated they were.

The score that you need to attain will vary based on the area. A passing score will be around 460, although there are some variations. A passing score in Virginia is 455 and 464 in Massachusetts. The minimum score required in most parts of Florida is 464, for instance. But the minimum is 457 in the Duval and Manatee County school districts.

Retaking the Test

What happens if you are unsuccessful the first time you take the ParaPro test? You have the right to retake the ParaPro test if needed, although you must wait 21 days. The questions will be randomly selected each time you complete the test.

There is no limit to how many times you can take the test. Updates to your score will be sent to the appropriate groups that you have indicated as recipients.

Conclusion

Being a paraprofessional is an important position and should not be taken for granted. Paraprofessionals support teachers and make it easier for them to do their jobs. Crucially, paraprofessionals are vital to helping students learn. They can assist them individually and offer tutoring. The services of a professional are particularly vital for children who have special learning needs and require additional assistance.

You must know what is involved in taking the ParaPro test. This is a very important test for your success in the field of education. Passing the test will confirm your ability to help students with many tasks and functions that they are required to master. The test includes questions about reading, writing and math, and covers critical concepts that must be learned in primary and secondary schools.

Knowing how the test is organized and how you can plan your studies to prepare for it will be vital to your success.

Made in the USA
Middletown, DE
09 February 2020